FUN PROJECTS FOR ALL SEASONS!

Published by

krause publications

700 East State Street • Iola, WI 54990-0001
715/445-2214 • FAX: 715/445-4087   www.krause.com

Please call or write for our free catalog of publications. To place an order
or obtain a free catalog, call our toll-free number (800) 258-0929. For
editorial comment or further information, use our regular business
telephone (715) 445-2214.

Designed by Jonathan Stein
Photography by Ross Hubbard, Kris Kandler, and Robert Best

Library of Congress Catalog Number: 98-87362
ISBN: 0-87341-940-5
Printed in the United States of America

INTRODUCTION

Year 'Round Fun 2 is truly a book for all seasons. You'll find projects for all of the holidays and celebrations you enjoy throughout the year. Some projects are quick and easy -- and others take a little longer. There are many projects that would be great to do with your whole family. Don't forget to ask Grandpa and Grandma to join in on the fun! They'd enjoy helping.

Have you thought about keeping a journal or scrapbook as you do the projects and activities? You'll have a great time looking at the photos and reading the journal later on. Some of your best memories when you grow up are the ones when you were making things. While Mom and Dad or Grandpa and Grandma are helping, ask them what they did for fun when they were kids. You might be surprised what they tell you! Ask what they made for the different holidays and add their stories to your journal. Maybe they'll teach you how to make one of their favorite projects if you ask them.

I've always enjoyed working with kids. I was a teacher in Minnesota and Illinois for 25 years and advised kids' organizations. We have five children of our own, and we've made lots of fun projects together over the years -- and still do!

I know you'll have a great time making the projects in this book -- all year 'round!

Noah and editor Bill tried on a couple of the quick-and-easy masks found in *Year 'Round Fun 2*. Check out page 85 to see what Noah really looks like.

Bill Stephani

SPRING

SUMMER

WHAT'S INSIDE

Love Bug 6

Elephant Heart Boxes 8

Valentine Boy & Girl 10

Leprechaun Pin 11

Leprechaun Candy Container 12

Easter Rabbit Door Hanger 14

Easter Egg Holders 16

Bunny Shelf Sitter 18

Kapok Easter Cards 20

Easter Bunny Magnet or Pin 21

Birdhouse Plant Poke or Magnet 22

Key Holder & Key Chains 24

Birdhouse Frame 26

Cartoon into Spring 28

Uncle Sam Magnet or Pin 29

Uncle Sam Door Hanger 30

Felt Tepee 32

Glow-in-the-Dark Lighthouse 34

Suede Covered Boxes 36

Daniel & the Lion 38

Puppy Picture Frame 40

Picket Fence Frame 42

Seashore Canister Set 43

Mosaic Fish Treasure Box 44

Butterfly Necklace & Barrette 45

Windmill Skit 46

Completed Dutch Windmill 48

Dutch Windmill Cutout 49

Paper Boomerangs 58

Make Your Own Hygrometer 60

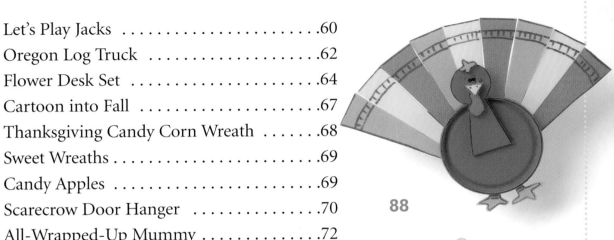

FALL

Let's Play Jacks 60
Oregon Log Truck 62
Flower Desk Set 64
Cartoon into Fall 67
Thanksgiving Candy Corn Wreath 68
Sweet Wreaths 69
Candy Apples 69
Scarecrow Door Hanger 70
All-Wrapped-Up Mummy 72
Halloween Masks 74
Halloween Party Favors 80
Vampire Candy Can 82
Frankenstein Treat Holder 83
Bat Pin 83
Boo Buddies Tee Shirt 84
Paper-Strip Pumpkin 86
Clay Pot Turkey 87
Turkey Magnet 88
Pilgrim & Indian Clothespin Dolls 89

WINTER

Snowman Candle Holder 92
Santa Spoon Ornament 93
Santa Door Hanger 94
Hanukkah Card Holder 96
Milk Bottle Nativity 98
Foam Ornament Set 100
Santa Ring Toss Game 102
Milk Bottle Snowman 104

88

83

58

102

62

LOVE BUG

by Kathleen George

MATERIALS

- Plastic foam shapes*: 3⅞" egg, 2½" ball, 1½" ball, three 1" balls
- Bright rose acrylic paint
- 7"x18" heart pattern fabric
- 7"x9" fusible interfacing
- Scrap of pink foam for mouth
- Gold dimensional glitter paint
- Gold glitter glue
- 4 violet chenille stems
- 8" of 1" grosgrain ribbon
- ½" pink pom pom
- ½"x¾" oval wiggle eyes
- Hot glue gun and glue stick
- Thick craft glue
- Glass, paintbrush, serrated kitchen knife, straight pins, toothpicks, wire cutter, wooden skewer

Styrofoam® plastic foam shapes were used for this project.

INSTRUCTIONS

☺ Adult supervision is needed when using serrated knife and hot glue gun.

☺ Trace and cut out pattern. Follow directions.

1 Use knife to cut a slice from fat end of egg so it will sit. Twist 2" ball on top of egg until it fits tightly. Hot glue together. For cheeks, cut 1½" ball in half. Twist the cut edges against head until they fit. Hot glue together. For feet, cut 1" balls in half. Paint all foam pieces rose. ***Hint:*** *Push wooden skewer into bottom of large pieces to hold while painting. Place skewer in heavy glass while paint dries. Push smaller pieces on toothpick while painting. Stick toothpicks in scrap of foam while paint dries.*

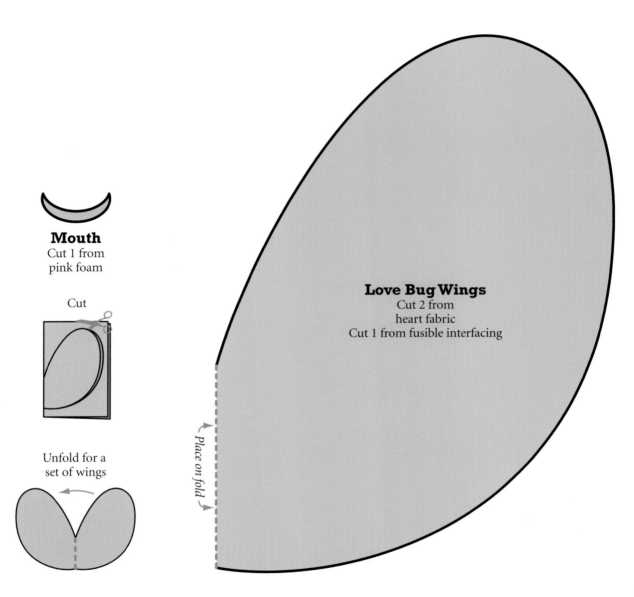

Mouth
Cut 1 from
pink foam

Cut

Unfold for a
set of wings

Love Bug Wings
Cut 2 from
heart fabric
Cut 1 from fusible interfacing

Place on fold

2 Follow manufacturer's directions to apply fusible interfacing on back of one set of wings. Fuse second set of wings on back of first. Squeeze a thin line of glitter paint around edge of wings. Set aside to dry.

3 For antenna, cut four small hearts from scraps of fabric. Cut two 3" chenille stems. Bend stems crooked. Glue hearts together, sandwiching end of stem between them. Squeeze a thin line of glitter paint around edge of hearts. Repeat for other antenna. Set aside to dry.

4 See photo and glue on wiggle eyes and pom pom nose. Cut a smile mouth from pink foam. Glue mouth on face. Glue wings on back of bug. Hold mouth and wings on with straight pins. Dip end of antenna in glue and push into top of head. Repeat for other antenna.

Cut six 3" chenille stems. Dip ends in glue. Push one end into curved side of a foot. Push other end into body. Repeat for all legs. Bend legs in half in different directions.

Tie ribbon in a bow. Cut ribbon ends at a slant. Glue bow on neck. Cut out six small fabric hearts; glue on bottom of feet. Cut two medium hearts; glue on cheeks. Cut a large heart; glue on chest. Apply glitter glue around hearts on wings, bottoms of feet, cheeks, chest, and antennae. ■

ELEPHANT HEART BOXES

by Mary Ayres

MATERIALS FOR EACH

- ▶ 1½"x3¼"x3¼" papier mâché heart box*
- ▶ Two 2" wood hearts*
- ▶ Wood craft shapes*: ⅞" hearts, two 1½" hearts, craft stick mini
- ▶ Acrylic paint*: White Wash, True Red, Baby Pink, Peony Pink
- ▶ #6 and #8 round paintbrushes
- ▶ Twin tip (fine & bullet) black permanent marker
- ▶ Thick craft glue
- ▶ Paper towel, pencil, tracing paper

The following products were used for this project: Decorator & Craft Corporation heart box · Lara's Crafts wood hearts · Forster® Woodsies™ wood craft shapes · DecoArt™ Americana™ acrylic paint · ZIG® Memory System™ marker.

PAINTING TIPS

DRY BRUSH - Dip dry round bristle brush in paint and wipe off on paper towel until brush is almost dry. Wipe brush across edges for light shading.

ROUGING - Dip dry round bristle brush in paint and wipe off on paper towel until brush is almost completely dry with no brush strokes showing. Wipe brush across cheeks in circular motion.

DOTS - Dip end of brush handle into fresh puddle of paint and dot on project. Repeat for each dot to keep the same size.

INSTRUCTIONS
DARK PINK ELEPHANT

1 Paint box, ears, and trunk Peony Pink. Dry brush edges with White Wash.

2 For inside ears, paint 1½" heart with White Wash. Dry brush edges with Baby Pink. Dot evenly spaced Baby Pink dots on inside ears.

3 Paint ⅞" heart Baby Pink. Dry brush edges with Peony Pink. Use fine point of marker to write "be mine" on heart.

4 Transfer face to box lid. Rouge cheeks with True Red. Draw eyes and a dot at end of trunk with black

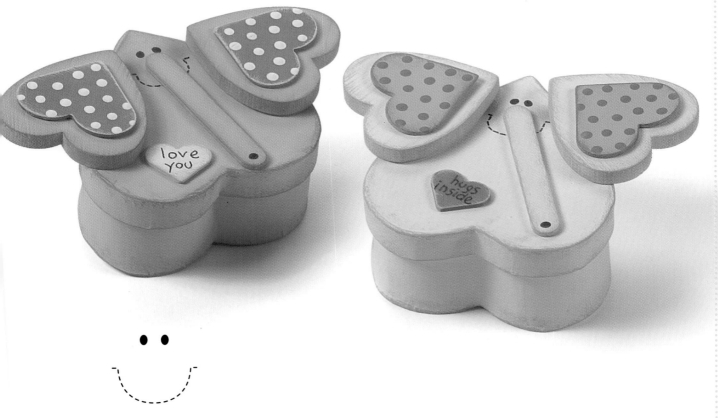

Figure 1

marker, using side of bullet tip. Use fine tip of marker to draw mouth.

5 Glue inside ears on ears. Glue ears, trunk, and heart with words on top of box lid.

LIGHT PINK ELEPHANT

1 Paint box, ears, and trunk Baby Pink. Dry brush edges Peony Pink.

2 For inside ears, paint 1½" heart with Peony Pink. Dry brush edges White Wash. Dot evenly spaced White Wash dots on inside ears.

3 Paint ⅞" heart with White Wash. Dry brush edges with Baby Pink.

Use fine point of marker to write "love you" on heart.

4 Transfer face to box lid. Rouge cheeks with True Red. Draw eyes and a dot at end of trunk with black marker, using side of bullet tip. Use fine tip of marker to draw mouth.

5 Glue inside ears on ears. Glue ears, trunk, and heart with words on top of box lid.

WHITE ELEPHANT

1 Paint box, ears, and trunk with White Wash. Dry brush edges Baby Pink.

2 For inside ears, paint 1½" heart Baby Pink. Dry brush edges with Peony Pink. Dot evenly spaced Peony Pink dots on inside ears.

3 Paint ⅞" heart Peony Pink. Dry brush edges with White Wash. Use fine point of marker to write "hugs inside" on heart.

4 Transfer face to box lid. Rouge cheeks with True Red. Draw eyes and a dot at end of trunk with black marker, using side of bullet tip. Use fine tip of marker to draw mouth.

5 Glue inside ears on ears. Glue ears, trunk, and heart with words on top of box lid. ■

VALENTINE BOY & GIRL

by Mary Ayres

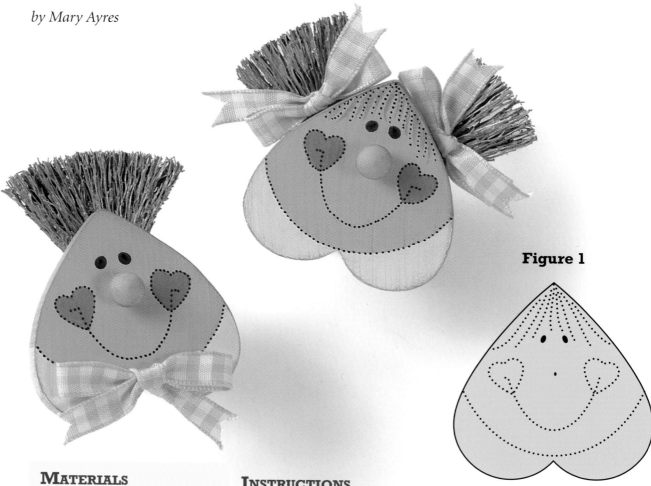

Figure 1

MATERIALS

- Two 2" wood hearts
- Two ¼" wood furniture buttons
- Three 3" flat straw brooms
- Acrylic paint*: White Wash, Baby Pink, Peony Pink, Shimmering Silver
- Paintbrushes: #6 round, #6 soft round, liner
- 18" length of ¼" pink check ribbon
- Twin tip (fine & bullet) black permanent marker
- Two pin backs: ¾", 1½"
- Thick craft glue
- Graphite paper, paper towels, pencil, scissors

* The following products were used for this project: Lara's Crafts wood hearts · DecoArt™ Americana™ acrylic paint · ZIG® Memory System™ writer.

INSTRUCTIONS

☺ See photo for design detail.

☺ To dry brush, dip a dry round bristle brush in paint and wipe off on a paper towel until brush is almost dry. Wipe brush across edges for light shading.

GIRL

1 See Figure 1. Use graphite paper to transfer collar line and heart cheeks to wood heart. Paint collar White Wash. Paint cheeks Peony Pink. Paint rest of wood heart and furniture button nose Baby Pink. Dry brush heart and nose edges Peony Pink.

2 Use graphite paper to transfer hair, eyes, and mouth to wood heart. Paint Shimmering Silver hair. Draw eyes with black marker, using side of bullet tip. Use fine tip of marker to add hair dots, outline cheeks and top edge of collar, and add smiling dot mouth. For nose, glue wood button between cheeks.

3 For hair, remove handles from two brooms. Twist handles to break glue bond and pull out. Paint hair Shimmering Silver. Glue hair on back of head on both sides. Cut two 6" pieces pink check ribbon. (Save last piece of ribbon for boy.) Tie in two small bows with even ends. Trim ribbon ends in a "v." Glue bows on sides of head in front of hair. Let dry. Glue 1½" pin back horizontally on back of girl on hair.

BOY

1 See photo. Make boy same as for girl except boy's hair uses one broom and has one bow glued on collar. ■

LEPRECHAUN PIN

by Helen Rafson

Hat
Cut 1 from
green foam

Hatband
Cut 1 from
dark green foam

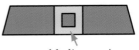

gold glitter paint

Eyebrow
Cut 2 from
orange foam

Face
Cut 1 from
white foam

Ear
Cut 2 from
white foam

Beard
Cut 1 from
orange foam

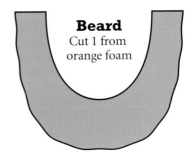

**Add a little
shamrock or clover
of your own.**

MATERIALS
- Craft foam: green, dark green, white, orange
- Acrylic paint: black, flesh, red, dark green
- Black fine-tip permanent marker
- Pink powder makeup blush
- Gold glitter pen
- Pinking shears
- 1¼" pinback
- Craft foam glue*
- Cotton swab, pencil, scissors, small paintbrush, toothpick

* Beacon Chemical Co. craft foam glue was used for this project.

INSTRUCTIONS

1 Trace patterns on craft foam. Cut out. Cut outer edge of beard with pinking shears.

2 Use marker to draw a dotted line close to edge of hat. Use gold glitter pen to make buckle on hatband. When dry, glue hatband on hat.

3 Glue beard on face. Glue ears on beard. Glue eyebrows on face. Dip end of paintbrush in black paint. Dot two eyes on face. Clean end of paintbrush and dip it into flesh paint. Dot nose on face. When dry, dip end of toothpick in white paint; add tiny white highlight dots on eyes. Use marker to draw mouth. Dip end of paintbrush in red paint and add a dot at each end of mouth. Use cotton swab to add blush on cheeks.

4 For shamrocks, dip end of paintbrush in dark green paint and make three dots on beard and three dots on hat. Paint a dark green stem on each shamrock. When dry, outline shamrocks with marker.

5 Glue bottom edge of hat on top edge of face. Glue pinback on back of leprechaun. ■

LEPRECHAUN CANDY CONTAINER

by Helen Rafson

MATERIALS

- Empty Pringles® container
- Felt: green, gold, pink, dark pink, orange
- Green craft foam
- Two 18mm wiggle eyes
- Acrylic paint: orange, green
- Matte acrylic spray
- Paint primer
- Black embroidery floss
- 9⅝" length of 1" black grosgrain ribbon
- 28⅝" length of 1" green grosgrain ribbon
- Water soluble marker
- Thick craft glue
- Needle, paintbrush, pencil, ruler

INSTRUCTIONS

☺   Let paint dry between coats.

1 Clean and dry Pringles container. Paint a coat of primer around outside of container.

2 Draw a line around container 3" down from top. Paint 2 coats of orange below line. Paint 2 coats of green above line. Spray container with matte acrylic.

3 Trace and cut out patterns. Follow directions on patterns. Glue cheeks on face. Use marker to draw mouth lines to be stitched. For stitching mouth, use 6 strands of floss to stitch mouth as shown in photo.

4 Glue eyes, nose, and eyebrows on face. Glue face on container.

5 Glue green ribbon around bottom. Glue on beard leaving edges unglued so it will stand out. Glue brim on at line. Glue black ribbon around hat as shown. Glue on buckle.

6 Glue green felt on top of plastic cap. Cut ⅜"x10¼" strip of green felt. Glue strip around edge of cap.

7 Make a bow with green ribbon. Cut ends in a "v". Glue bow on Leprechaun as shown in photo. ■

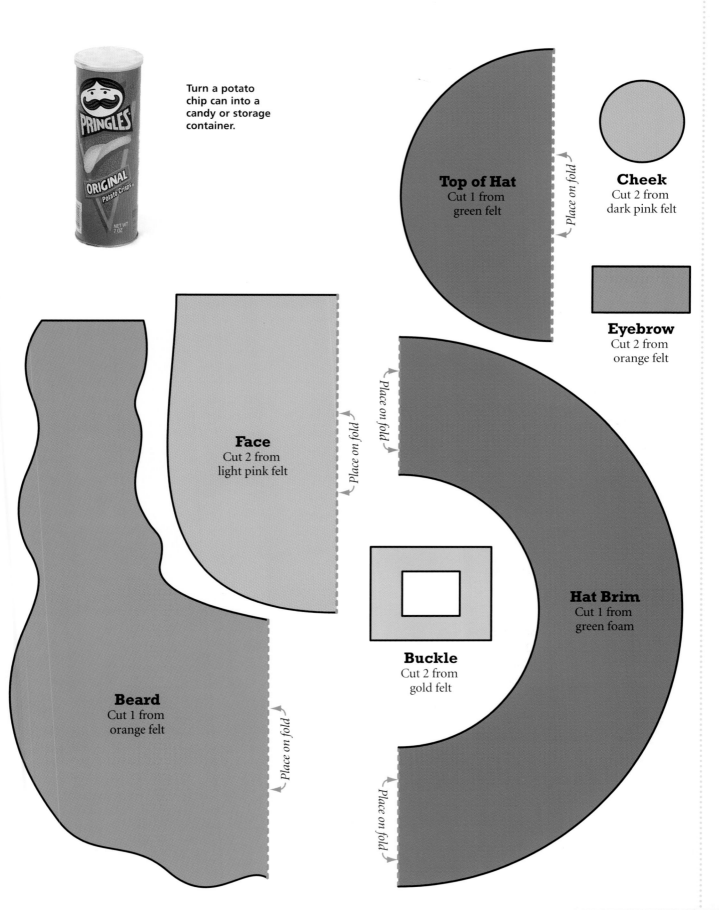

Turn a potato chip can into a candy or storage container.

Top of Hat
Cut 1 from
green felt

Place on fold

Cheek
Cut 2 from
dark pink felt

Eyebrow
Cut 2 from
orange felt

Face
Cut 2 from
light pink felt

Place on fold

Place on fold

Hat Brim
Cut 1 from
green foam

Buckle
Cut 2 from
gold felt

Beard
Cut 1 from
orange felt

Place on fold

Place on fold

Easter Rabbit Door Hanger

by Debi Goldfisher

MATERIALS

- 3"x9½" wood door hanger
- Felt*: 8"x9" white, 3"x3" yellow, 3"x3" dark pink
- Lemon Custard acrylic paint*
- Acrylic spray sealer
- #8 flat paintbrush
- Embroidery floss: black, yellow, pink
- 6" of ⅜" floral ribbon
- 21" of ³⁄₁₆" pink ribbon
- Polyester fiberfill
- Two ½" diameter pink buttons
- Two black seed beads
- 1½" straw basket
- Black fine-line permanent marker
- Thick craft glue
- Brown paper bag, needle, paper plate, pencil, sandpaper, scissors, straight pins, toothpick, tracing paper, water container

* The following products were used for this project: Kunin Classic Rainbow™ Felt · Plaid FolkArt® acrylic paint.

INSTRUCTIONS

☺ Trace and cut out patterns. Follow directions.

☺ Use two strands of floss for all stitching.

1 Sand door hanger. Paint front and edges with two coats Lemon Custard. Use marker to draw stitch lines around edges of doorknob opening and outside edges of hanger. Spray with a coat of acrylic sealer. Rub surface with a piece of paper bag to smooth.

2 Glue nose on face of one rabbit piece. See Figure 1. Use black floss to sew a straight stitch mouth from bottom point of nose. Sew straight stitch whiskers through nose.

3 With wrong sides together, pin rabbit bodies together. Sew running stitch around edges with pink floss, leaving an opening for stuffing. Stuff lightly with fiberfill before sewing closed.

4 For eyes, glue beads on face, using toothpick to apply glue. Glue ear centers on middle of each ear.

5 Cut a 5" piece of pink ribbon; wrap around neck and glue together in back. Cut an 8" piece of ribbon and tie into a bow. Glue bow on center front of neck ribbon.

6 Cut floral ribbon in half. Pin one piece on one pink egg. Pin two pink eggs together, wrong sides together. Sew together with yellow floss and a running stitch around outer edge, tucking ribbon ends between felt layers. Leave an opening for stuffing. Stuff egg lightly. Sew across opening. Repeat for yellow egg, using pink floss.

7 See photo. Glue rabbit on front of door hanger below knob opening. Glue eggs on front of body. Tie remaining piece of ribbon into a bow and glue on basket. Glue basket on base of rabbit. Glue a button on each top corner of door hanger.

GLUING TIPS

▶ For pieces requiring identical fronts and backs, such as snowman and rabbit, glue two layers together for added body.

▶ For small objects such as beads, use a toothpick to apply glue. Glue should be placed where bead will be glued on figure, not on bead itself.

▶ Use a small piece of tape or paper clip to hold item in place until glue dries.

DOOR HANGER OPTION

▶ If a pre-cut wood door hanger is not available, one can be cut from stiff material such as craft foam, stiffened felt, or poster board.

▶ Select a color that will coordinate with felt figures.

▶ The paint and painting supplies on materials list will no longer be needed for project.

NO-SEW METHOD

To simplify this project for younger crafters, felt figures can be glued together rather than sewn.

▶ The figures will be flat, not stuffed.

▶ Floss, fiberfill and sewing supplies on materials list will no longer be needed.

▶ The same pattern directions are used.

▶ The figure is assembled by gluing pieces together starting with the bottom layer and working up.

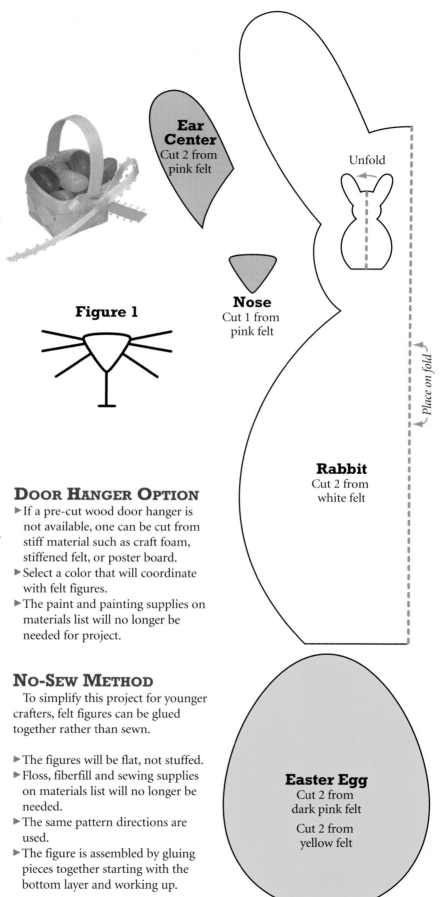

Figure 1

Ear Center
Cut 2 from pink felt

Nose
Cut 1 from pink felt

Unfold

Place on fold

Rabbit
Cut 2 from white felt

Easter Egg
Cut 2 from dark pink felt

Cut 2 from yellow felt

BUNNIES AND CHICK EASTER EGGS FAVORS

by Lisa Marto Weber

MATERIALS

- 1 sheet super thick white craft foam*
- Scrap of orange thin craft foam
- Wood craft shapes*: 2 small hearts, 1 small circle
- Acrylic paint*: Light Fuchsia, Medium Fuchsia, White, True Turquoise, True Orange, Electric Blue, Medium Blue
- Pacific Blue fabric writer*
- Wood markers*: Yellow, Forget-Me-Not Blue
- Gloss varnish
- Ultra-fine black permanent marker
- 10 yellow feathers
- 3 plastic Easter eggs
- Sea sponge
- Craft knife
- Thick craft glue*
- Paintbrushes, paper plate, pencil, tracing paper, toothpicks

* *The following products were used for this project: Darice® Super Thick Foamies · Aleene's™ Premium-Coat acrylic paint, Enhancers varnish, glue · Scribbles 3-D Crystal Gel Fabric Writer · ZIG® Wood Craft Markers · Forster® Woodsies™ wood craft shapes.*

INSTRUCTIONS

- ☺ Adult supervision is needed when using craft knife.
- ☺ Trace and cut out patterns. Follow directions.
- ☺ Let paint and markers dry completely after each coat.

1 Use craft knife to carefully cut bunny or chick and base from craft foam.

2 For girl bunny, pour small puddles of Light Fuchsia, Medium Fuchsia, and White on paper plate. Dip sea sponge in all three colors and sponge on bunny back, front, and base.

Trace face onto bunny. Go over pencil lines with black permanent marker. Color mouth with marker. Paint eyes white on top and turquoise on bottom. Paint nose Medium Fuchsia. Dip end of toothpick in white and dot a small white highlight on turquoise part of eye. Use marker to add "stitch lines" close to edge of body. Glue base on center bottom of back of bunny.

3 For boy bunny, use Forget-Me-Not Blue marker to color bunny and base. Trace and paint face same as for girl bunny, except use Pacific Blue for eyes. Dip toothpick in white and add small highlight on eyes and corner of mouth. Dip end of toothpick in Pacific Blue to make dots all over boy bunny's body. Glue base on center bottom of back of bunny.

4 For chick, use yellow marker to color chick and base. Trace and paint eyes same as for boy bunny. Fold beak in half. Put a tiny dot of glue inside beak, but don't glue beak completely closed. Hold until glue dries. Put glue on fold and hold on chick's face until dry.

Paint wood hearts and circles Electric Blue. Use toothpick and Medium Blue to add dots to all wood pieces. See Figure 1. For bow tie, lay hearts with points touching. Glue circle over points on both hearts. Glue bow tie on chick's neck.

Glue feathers on bottom of chick's body. Glue base on center bottom of back of chick.

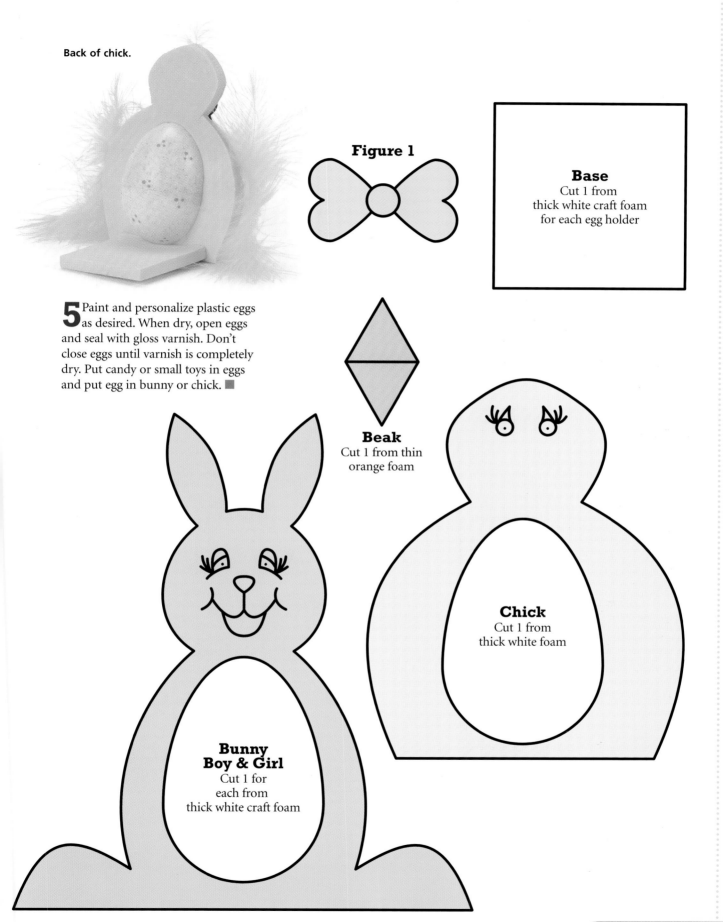

Back of chick.

Figure 1

Base
Cut 1 from
thick white craft foam
for each egg holder

5 Paint and personalize plastic eggs as desired. When dry, open eggs and seal with gloss varnish. Don't close eggs until varnish is completely dry. Put candy or small toys in eggs and put egg in bunny or chick. ■

Beak
Cut 1 from thin
orange foam

Chick
Cut 1 from
thick white foam

**Bunny
Boy & Girl**
Cut 1 for
each from
thick white craft foam

BUNNY SHELF SITTER

by Sandy Parpart

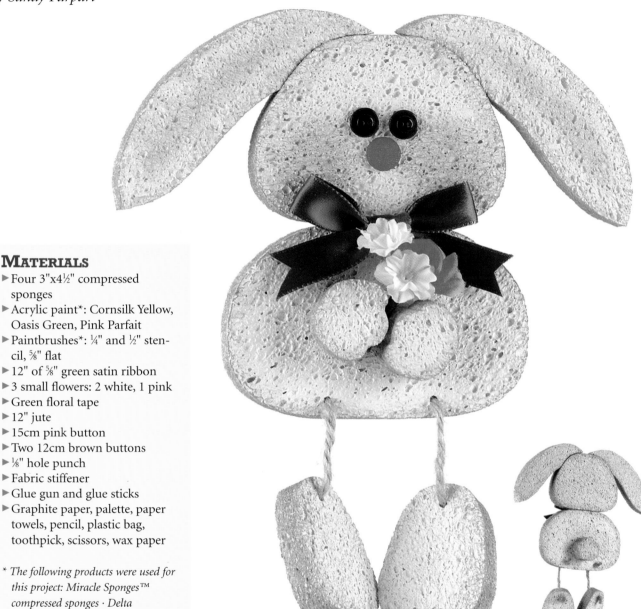

Backside of bunny

MATERIALS

- ▶ Four 3"x4½" compressed sponges
- ▶ Acrylic paint*: Cornsilk Yellow, Oasis Green, Pink Parfait
- ▶ Paintbrushes*: ¼" and ½" stencil, ⅝" flat
- ▶ 12" of ⅝" green satin ribbon
- ▶ 3 small flowers: 2 white, 1 pink
- ▶ Green floral tape
- ▶ 12" jute
- ▶ 15cm pink button
- ▶ Two 12cm brown buttons
- ▶ ⅛" hole punch
- ▶ Fabric stiffener
- ▶ Glue gun and glue sticks
- ▶ Graphite paper, palette, paper towels, pencil, plastic bag, toothpick, scissors, wax paper

* The following products were used for this project: Miracle Sponges™ compressed sponges · Delta Ceramcoat® acrylic paint and Stencil Magic® stencil brushes · Loew-Cornell® paintbrush.

INSTRUCTIONS

1 Use graphite paper to transfer patterns on compressed sponges. Cut out. Punch holes in sponge pieces as shown on pattern. Dip sponge into water, squeeze out excess, then squeeze between paper towels until almost dry.

2 Pour fabric stiffener into plastic bag. To stiffen bunny pieces, put them into baggie, one piece at a time. Completely saturate bunny pieces by squeezing the baggie. Squeeze excess fabric stiffener from pieces and lay on wax paper to dry. Add more fabric stiffener to bag as needed.

3 Use flat brush to paint all bunny pieces with two coats Cornsilk Yellow. Let paint dry between coats. Use stencil brush and Oasis Green to dry brush around edges of bunny pieces. ***Note:*** *To dry brush, dip stencil brush into paint, rub brush on paper towel until nearly dry. Rub stencil brush*

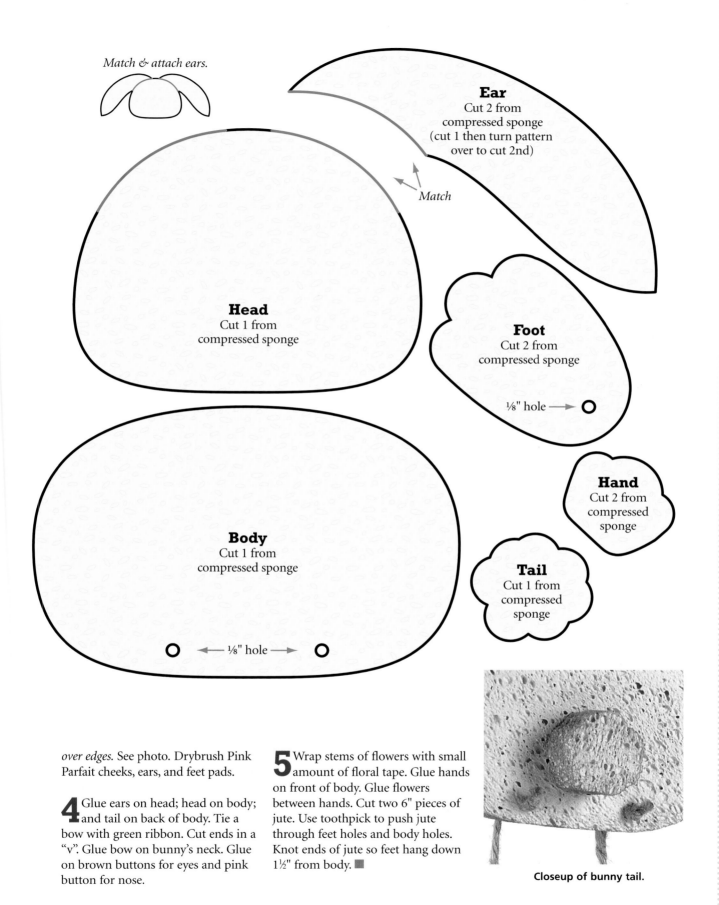

Match & attach ears.

Ear
Cut 2 from
compressed sponge
(cut 1 then turn pattern
over to cut 2nd)

Match

Head
Cut 1 from
compressed sponge

Foot
Cut 2 from
compressed sponge

⅛" hole →

Hand
Cut 2 from
compressed
sponge

Body
Cut 1 from
compressed sponge

← ⅛" hole →

Tail
Cut 1 from
compressed
sponge

over edges. See photo. Drybrush Pink Parfait cheeks, ears, and feet pads.

4 Glue ears on head; head on body; and tail on back of body. Tie a bow with green ribbon. Cut ends in a "v". Glue bow on bunny's neck. Glue on brown buttons for eyes and pink button for nose.

5 Wrap stems of flowers with small amount of floral tape. Glue hands on front of body. Glue flowers between hands. Cut two 6" pieces of jute. Use toothpick to push jute through feet holes and body holes. Knot ends of jute so feet hang down 1½" from body. ▪

Closeup of bunny tail.

EASTER CARDS

by Charlene Messerle

MATERIALS

- ► 7"x10" card stock, color of your choice
- ► Assorted small artificial flowers and buds
- ► 3 green leaves, assorted sizes
- ► Small amount of Spanish moss
- ► Fabric glue*
- ► Pencil, toothpicks, tracing paper, wax paper

Fabri-Tac™ glue was used for this project.

INSTRUCTIONS

1 Transfer cross to front of card. Print a Bible verse or a saying on inside of card. Some suggestions are:
- · He Is Risen!
- · Happy Easter
- · Christ is King

2 Spread wax paper on table. Use toothpick to put glue on small pieces of Spanish moss. Glue inside outline of cross. Fill in entire cross.

3 Cut off flower stems close to blossom. Pour a little glue on wax paper. Dip bottom of flower in glue and tuck in Spanish moss. Glue leaves around flowers. ■

Glue Spanish moss and flowers in the shape of a cross.

EASTER BUNNY MAGNET OR PIN

by Helen L. Rafson

MATERIALS

- ▶ Craft spoon*
- ▶ 2"x2" white craft foam
- ▶ Acrylic paint: black and white
- ▶ Paintbrush
- ▶ 3" grey embroidery floss
- ▶ 6" of ¼" light blue satin ribbon
- ▶ Pom poms: two 7mm white, one 5mm pink
- ▶ Four ½" white buttons
- ▶ Pink powder makeup blush
- ▶ Black permanent fine-tip marker
- ▶ Magnet or pinback
- ▶ Thick craft glue
- ▶ Cotton swab, pencil, ruler, scissors, straight pin, toothpick, tracing paper

* Forster® Woodsies™ craft spoon was used for this project.

INSTRUCTIONS

- ☺ Trace and cut out pattern. Follow directions.
- ☺ Let paint dry completely after each coat.

1 Paint spoon with 2 or 3 coats of white paint. Use marker to draw lines around edge of spoon and ears. Use cotton swab to apply blush on ears.

2 For nose, glue pink pom pom in center of spoon. Dip handle end of paintbrush in black paint and dot 2 eyes above nose. Dip tip of toothpick in white paint and add tiny highlights in eyes.

3 For whiskers, tie a knot in middle of embroidery floss. Use straight pin to separate strands of floss. Glue under nose. Trim ends. Glue teeth under whiskers. For cheeks, glue white pom poms under nose, on top of teeth and whiskers.

4 Tie ribbon in a bow. Cut ends at a slant. Mix 1 drop glue with 1 drop water. Use finger to dab glue/water mix on cut end of ribbon so it doesn't fray. Let dry. Glue bow on bunny's neck. Glue buttons under bow. Glue magnet or pinback on back of spoon. ∎

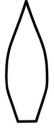

Ear
Cut 2 from white foam

Tooth
Cut 2 from white foam

BIRDHOUSE PLANT POKE OR MAGNET

by Helen Rafson

MATERIALS FOR BOTH
- ▶ Photograph
- ▶ 5"x5" tan felt*
- ▶ 2 print fabrics, each 5"x5"
- ▶ 5"x5" fusible web
- ▶ Tan embroidery floss*
- ▶ ⅛" dowel: 12" length for plant poke, 4½" length for magnet
- ▶ 3 small buttons
- ▶ Several strands raffia
- ▶ 4½" magnet strip
- ▶ Fabric glue
- ▶ Iron, matching thread, needle, pencil, pinking shears, pins, scissors, tracing paper

* The following products were used for this project: Kunin Felt · DMC #437 embroidery floss · Aleene's Fusible Web.

INSTRUCTIONS

☺ Adult supervision is needed when using iron.

☺ Trace and cut out patterns. Follow directions.

1 Follow manufacturer's directions to fuse webbing on back of all fabrics. Cut out patterns. Pink edges of roof for magnet if desired.

2 Cut photograph slightly larger than birdhouse opening. Glue photograph in birdhouse opening. Let dry. Glue birdhouse on felt. Glue roof on birdhouse.

3 See photo. Sew on buttons. Pin felt pieces together. Thread three

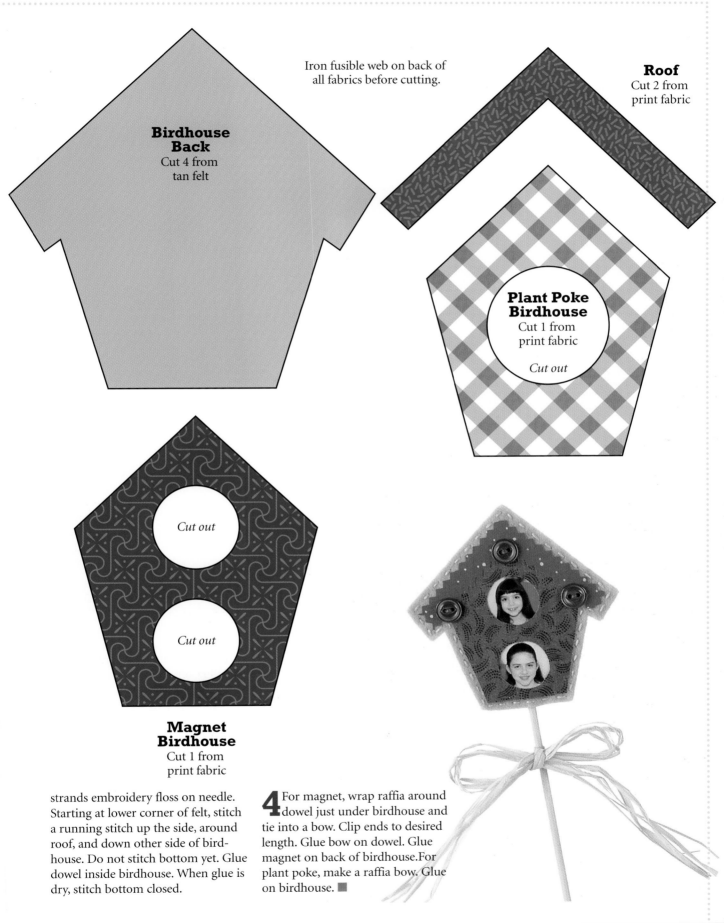

Iron fusible web on back of
all fabrics before cutting.

**Birdhouse
Back**
Cut 4 from
tan felt

Roof
Cut 2 from
print fabric

**Plant Poke
Birdhouse**
Cut 1 from
print fabric

Cut out

Cut out

Cut out

**Magnet
Birdhouse**
Cut 1 from
print fabric

strands embroidery floss on needle.
Starting at lower corner of felt, stitch
a running stitch up the side, around
roof, and down other side of birdhouse. Do not stitch bottom yet. Glue
dowel inside birdhouse. When glue is
dry, stitch bottom closed.

4 For magnet, wrap raffia around
dowel just under birdhouse and
tie into a bow. Clip ends to desired
length. Glue bow on dowel. Glue
magnet on back of birdhouse. For
plant poke, make a raffia bow. Glue
on birdhouse. ■

KEY HOLDER & KEY CHAINS

by Barbara Bennett

MATERIALS

- 2 cubes white clay
- ¼ cube of clay: turquoise, pink, lime, yellow
- 3 link chains
- 4 cup screws
- Two 2" eye pins
- Pallet knife, rolling pin, toothpicks, pencil, tracing paper, scissors, aluminum foil-lined baking sheet, oven

INSTRUCTIONS

☺ Adult supervision is needed when using an oven.

1 Trace patterns onto tracing paper and cut out.

2 Cover a baking sheet with aluminum foil and form the ornament on it.

3 Knead modeling compound to a pliable consistency. Press white clay to ³⁄₁₆" thickness using rolling pin for rectangle back of key holder. Roll clay to ¼" thickness to cut out heart, circle, and square key chains.

4 Using assorted colors of clay, form ¼" snakes long enough to drape around circumference of key holder

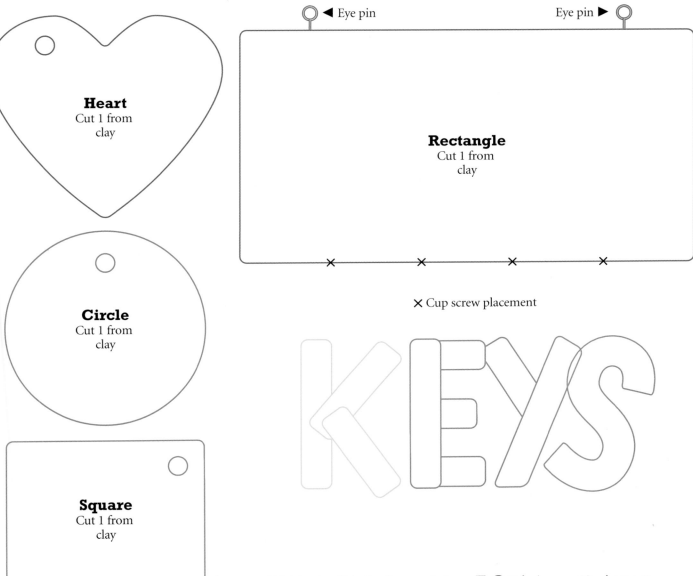

Heart
Cut 1 from
clay

Circle
Cut 1 from
clay

Square
Cut 1 from
clay

◀ Eye pin   Eye pin ▶

Rectangle
Cut 1 from
clay

✕ Cup screw placement

and around all key chains. Use pallet knife to press edges gently together. Join seams together and smooth raw edges with fingers.

5 For the letters KEYS, roll a snake ¼" thick. Lay snake on pattern, cutting and overlapping ends of clay with pallet knife. Continue this technique for each letter, alternating clay colors. Transfer letters to center of key holder and gently press letters together.

6 Make tiny ⅛" balls of assorted clay colors and place around edging of plaque.

7 Insert 2 eye pins in top edge of plaque. Insert 4 cup screws in bottom edge as indicated on pattern.

8 Names on key chains are 1/16" thick snakes of coordinating clay colors. Shape your name or MOM and DAD and press gently in place.

9 Use a toothpick to pierce a hole in each key chain as indicated on patterns.

10 Bake in oven 20 minutes at 225°. Remove and let cool thoroughly. Clay may feel soft when removed from oven but will harden as it cools.

11 After all clay pieces are completely cool, thread ribbon through eye pins at top of hanger to put on wall.

12 Insert link chains through hole in each key chain to hang key on. ∎

BIRDHOUSE FRAME

by Debi Goldfisher

MATERIALS

- 7"x9" wood frame (4"x6" opening)*
- Green and blue acrylic paint*
- Acrylic spray sealer*
- Stiffened felt*: yellow, green, burgundy, white
- Fabric scraps
- ½ yard ⅛" gold ribbon
- Eight ½" buttons: four blue, two burgundy, two yellow
- ¼" diameter tree twigs: two 7" lengths, eight 2½" lengths
- Fine-line black marker
- Flat paintbrush
- Thick craft glue
- Brown paper bag, craft stick, paper plate, pencil, scissors, tracing paper, water container

The following products were used for this project: Walnut Hollow Small Frame · Plaid® FolkArt® acrylic paint · CPE Eazy Felt.

INSTRUCTIONS

☺ Trace and cut out patterns. Follow directions.

☺ Allow paint and sealer to dry thoroughly after each coat.

☺ See photo for color and detail placement.

1 Use paper plate for paint palette. For grass, across bottom of frame below opening. Paint edge, too. Paint rest of frame blue. Add another coat if necessary. Spray frame with acrylic sealer. Rub surface gently with a piece of brown paper bag to smooth surface.

2 Glue a fabric roof on each birdhouse. Center and glue a blue button on red and yellow birdhouses. Glue two burgundy buttons on green birdhouse. See Figure 1. Use black marker to draw face on cat. Glue heart on cat. Center and glue blue button on heart.

Figure 1

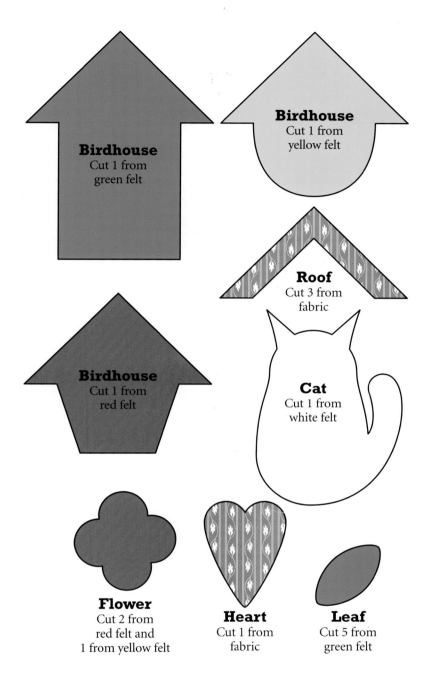

Birdhouse
Cut 1 from
green felt

Birdhouse
Cut 1 from
yellow felt

Roof
Cut 3 from
fabric

Birdhouse
Cut 1 from
red felt

Cat
Cut 1 from
white felt

Flower
Cut 2 from
red felt and
1 from yellow felt

Heart
Cut 1 from
fabric

Leaf
Cut 5 from
green felt

Did You Know?

► There is a seven-letter word in the English language that contains 10 words without rearranging any of its letters. This word is "therein," and the words within it are -- the, there, he, in, rein, her, here, ere, therein, herein.

► "Stewardesses" is the longest English word that is typed with only the left hand.

► The combination "ough" can be pronounced in nine different ways, and the following sentence contains them all. "A rough-coated, dough-faced, thoughtful ploughman strode through the streets of Scarborough; after falling into a slough, he coughed and hiccoughed."

► The only 15-letter word that can be spelled without repeating a letter is "uncopyrightable."

► "Underground" is the only word in the English language that begins and ends with the letters "und."

► The longest one-syllable word in the English language is "screeched."

► The symbol on the "pound" key is called an octothorpe.

3 Glue birdhouses on frame. For poles, cut ribbon to fit between bottom of birdhouse and ½" into grass. Glue ribbon ends down.

4 For fence, glue short twigs vertically on grass. Glue long twigs horizontally on top of short twigs. Glue flowers and leaves on frame above fence. Glue buttons in centers of flowers. Glue cat on fence. ■

Make Your Own Trail Mix

1 Decide on the ingredients you like best and pick them up at your grocery store. Many stores sell raisins, nuts, candy, and dried fruit in bulk quantities. While you're at the store, get some freezer bags, too.

2 In a large bowl or kettle, combine your favorite ingredients and mix well. Pour mixture into freezer bags and place in freezer. When you need a quick snack for the road, just grab a bag or two of your own trail mix.

3 Share with friends.

SPRING

LET'S DRAW SPRINGS!

BY: TRACEY PRESTON COOK

How many "spring" cartoons can you think of to draw? Can you think of a story to cartoon about a spring? Look how fun it could be to jump into puddles if you were a real spring! How about starting with a spring-shaped flower?

To cartoon your springs, you will have to "rough out" your spring shape using pencil lines and shapes. Start by trying the spring snake. First draw a rough pencil-line sketch of just the spring shape that will soon become a snake. Next, give the snake form by increasing the volume of the spring-shaped body until finally you add final details such as the eyes, tongue, and belly lines.

Now try cartooning the "spring-fish" character. Remember to start with a rough shape, and then fit your springs into the fish shape. If you draw the beginning shape well, the rest of the cartoon will turn out great!

DRAWING TIP:

To make the back of the loop look like it is behind the front part of the loop, try drawing the whole loop first. Then, erase only the portion of the loop in the back that should not be there (See the dotted line). **ERASE HERE**

What other "spring" cartoons can you think of?
How about a giraffe? Make up your own characters.

Uncle Sam Magnet or Pin

by Helen L. Rafson

Hat
Cut 1 from
white foam

Hat Brim
Cut 1 from
navy craft foam

MATERIALS

- Craft spoon*
- Craft foam: ¾"x1" white (hat), ¼"x1¼" navy (brim)
- Acrylic paint: white, flesh, black, navy
- Paintbrush
- Red satin ribbon: 3" of ⅛", 6" of ¼"
- Three ½" navy buttons
- 3 gold star sequins
- Pink powder makeup blush
- Black permanent fine-tip marker
- Magnet or pinback
- Thick craft glue
- Cotton swab, graphite paper, pencil, ruler, toothpick, tracing paper

* Forster® Woodsies™ craft spoon was used for this project.

INSTRUCTIONS

☺ Trace and cut out patterns. Follow directions.
☺ Let paint dry completely after each coat.

Figure 1

1 Glue top edge of brim on bottom edge of hat. Let dry. For stripes, cut 4 pieces of ⅛" ribbon ¾" long. See photo. Glue on hat. Glue 3 stars on brim. Let dry.

2 See Figure 1. Use graphite paper to transfer face on craft spoon. Paint body with 2 coats of navy. Paint face with 2 coats of flesh. Paint beard, mustache, goatee, and eyebrows with 2 coats of white. Dip handle end of paintbrush in black paint and dot 2 eyes on face. Dip end of toothpick in white and add tiny highlights on eyes.

3 See photo. Use marker to draw lines around body, face, eyebrows, nose, goatee, and mustache. Use cotton swab to apply blush on cheeks. Glue 3 buttons on body.

4 Tie ¼" red ribbon in a bow. Cut ends at a slant. Mix 1 drop of glue with 1 drop of water. Use finger to dab glue/water mix on cut end of ribbon so it doesn't fray. Let dry. Glue bow above buttons. Glue magnet or pinback on back of Uncle Sam. ■

UNCLE SAM DOOR HANGER

by Debi Goldfisher

MATERIALS

- 3"x9½" wood door hanger
- Felt*: 3"x4" ruby, 4"x5" white, 6"x6" royal blue, 7"x7" apricot
- Apple Spice acrylic paint*
- Acrylic spray sealer
- #8 flat paintbrush
- Red embroidery floss
- Polyester fiberfill
- Four ⅝" gold star buttons
- Seed beads: 2 black, 1 red
- 7mm gold bell
- Black fine-line permanent marker
- Thick craft glue
- Brown paper bag, needle, paper plate, pencil, sandpaper, scissors, straight pins, toothpick, tracing paper, water container

* The following products were used for this project: Kunin Classic Rainbow™ Felt · Plaid FolkArt® acrylic paint.

INSTRUCTIONS

Finished size: 3"x9½"

☺ Trace and cut out patterns. Follow directions.

1 Sand door hanger. Paint front and edges with two coats Apple Spice. Use marker to draw stitch lines around edges of doorknob opening and outside edges of hanger. Spray with a coat of acrylic sealer. Rub surface with a piece of paper bag to smooth.

2 Pin shirt on pants. Fit shirt and pants on body to be sure entire body will be covered. Use two strands embroidery floss to sew bottom edge of shirt on pants with running stitch. Sew clothing on body around outer edge of shirt and pants, leaving an opening for stuffing. Stuff lightly and sew opening closed.

3 Cut four ¼"x3" strips of ruby felt. Glue 2 strips on each pant leg. Trim ends if necessary. Glue feet on bottom of pants. Glue beard on face. Glue on seed bead eyes and red bead nose, using toothpick to apply glue. Glue hatband on hat. Glue hat on head. Glue star button on center of hatband and front of jacket.

4 Glue Uncle Sam on door hanger below hole. Glue bell on hand. Glue star buttons on top corners of door hanger. ■

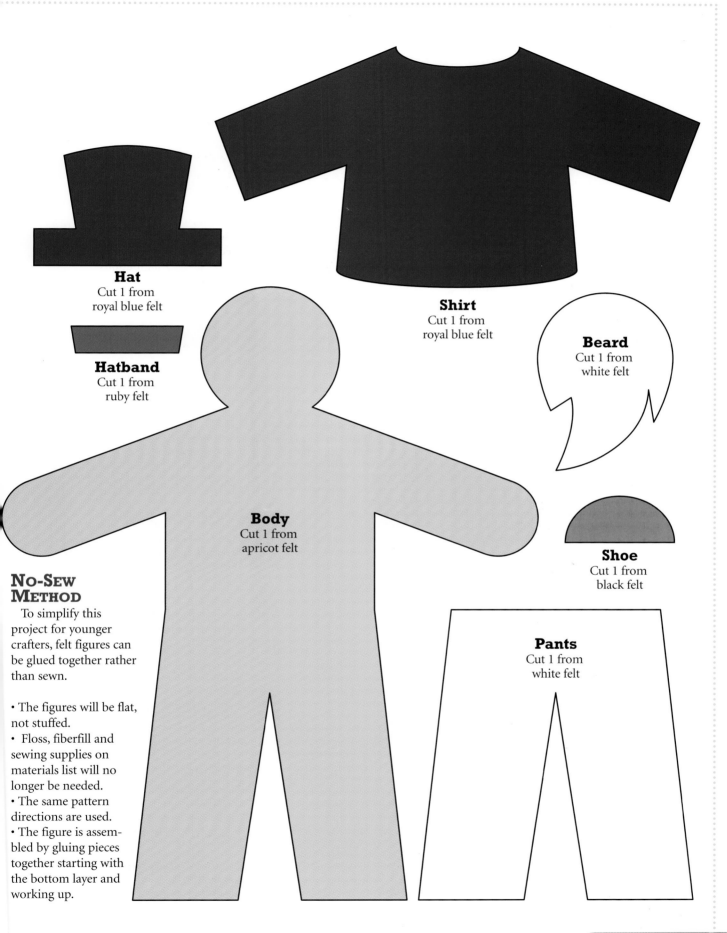

Hat
Cut 1 from
royal blue felt

Hatband
Cut 1 from
ruby felt

Shirt
Cut 1 from
royal blue felt

Beard
Cut 1 from
white felt

Body
Cut 1 from
apricot felt

Shoe
Cut 1 from
black felt

Pants
Cut 1 from
white felt

NO-SEW METHOD

To simplify this project for younger crafters, felt figures can be glued together rather than sewn.

• The figures will be flat, not stuffed.
• Floss, fiberfill and sewing supplies on materials list will no longer be needed.
• The same pattern directions are used.
• The figure is assembled by gluing pieces together starting with the bottom layer and working up.

CHILD'S TEPEE

by Lynn Farris

MATERIALS

▶ 60"-wide felt or foam backed fleece*: 1 yard each of three colors, 2 yards of another color for lining
▶ Matching thread
▶ 7 pieces of 6-foot long, ¾" diameter bamboo garden stakes *Optional: ¾" metal conduit as shown in photo*
▶ ⅔ yard of 2" Velcro®
▶ 3 yards giant chenille rickrack
▶ 2 yards coordinating chenille cord
▶ Large piece of craft paper or cardboard for pattern
▶ Air erasable marker.
▶ Ruler or tape measure, scissors, sewing machine, basic sewing supplies

Tempo Foam Backed Fleece fabric was used for tent. It is available only from the Fabric Club, P.O. Box 767670, Roswell, GA 30076. www.fabricclub.com. (800) FAB-CLUB (322-2582).

INSTRUCTIONS

☺ Adult help will be needed for this project.

Figure 1

1 See Figure 1. Draw a wedge shape which measures 9" wide across top, 24" across bottom, and 34" from top to bottom on large piece of paper. Cut out.

2 Trace patterns as close together as possible. Pattern may be turned upside down to fit on fabric. Trace pattern twice on each 1-yard piece of fabric leaving no more than 1" between shapes.

Trace pattern twice on 2-yard piece for door, saving extra fabric to make lining later.

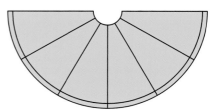

Figure 2

3 Cut out traced pieces. Arrange in alternating colors and sew six pieces together along long sides using ½" seam allowance. Shape will look like a half-circle. See Figure 2.

4 Pin sewn piece on remaining large piece of fabric with right sides together. Cut around outer edge. Sew

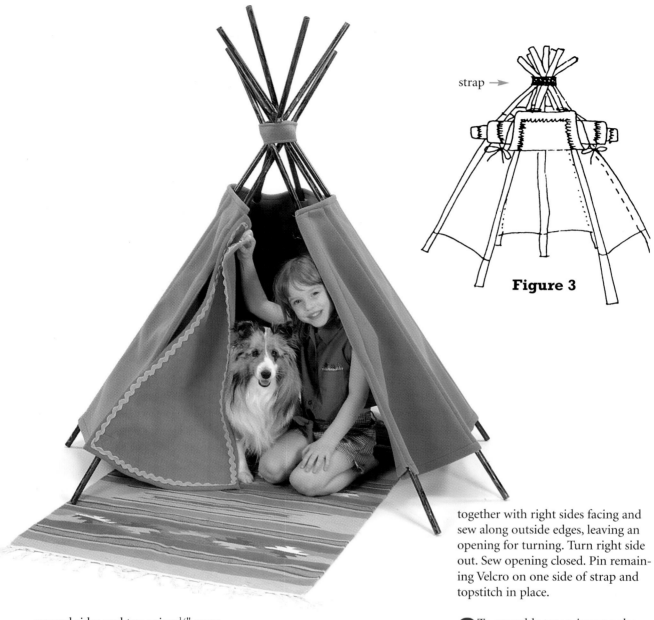

Figure 3

together with right sides facing and sew along outside edges, leaving an opening for turning. Turn right side out. Sew opening closed. Pin remaining Velcro on one side of strap and topstitch in place.

around sides and top using ½" seam allowance, leaving lower edge open. Turn up lower edge 1" and machine hem, leaving lining separate from cover.

5 Turn right side out. Pin lining to cover along seam of each section. Topstitch "in the ditch" from top to bottom at each seam. Sew a second row of stitching 2" to the left of each seam to form channels to hold poles. Cut a slit near top of each channel so top of pole can extend through cover.

6 For door, pin remaining two wedge-shaped pieces together with right sides facing. Sew around edges using ½" seam allowance, leaving a small area open along lower edge to turn. Turn right side out. Cut two 2" squares of Velcro and sew in upper inside corners. On outside, pin rickrack 1" from edge. Sew in place.

7 For strap to hold poles together, cut two 3"x18" pieces from remaining scraps of fabric. Pin

8 To assemble tepee, insert poles through channels and arrange so they extend the same distance from top and bottom of tepee. Gather poles together at top of tepee and wrap strap tightly about 6" from top. Stand tepee up and spread poles as far as they will go. Tepee will stand up best when placed on carpet rather than wood or linoleum floors.

See Figure 3. Roll up door and attach with Velcro to front opening of tepee. Tie chenille two cords to front poles, then around rolled door. ■

GLOW-IN-THE-DARK LIGHTHOUSE

by Barb Chauncey

"You are the light of the world" Matthew 5:13

MATERIALS

- ▶ 1"x6"x8" board
- ▶ 32-oz. plastic cup with snap-on lid
- ▶ 10-oz. clear plastic cup
- ▶ Jar rings, 1 wide-mouth, 1 regular
- ▶ Plastic berry basket
- ▶ Glass paint*: Ultra Black
- ▶ Acrylic paint*: Cadet Grey, Glo Up
- ▶ Gold finish*
- ▶ Black granite "Make It Stone"*
- ▶ ¾" flat paintbrush
- ▶ Medium-point black marker*
- ▶ 4 small self-adhesive felt circles
- ▶ Dried moss
- ▶ Small stones
- ▶ 8½"x11" piece paper
- ▶ Glue gun and glue sticks
- ▶ Thick craft glue
- ▶ Cotton swabs, disposable palette, masking tape, medium grit sandpaper, pencil, scissors, soft rag

* *The following products were used for this project: Delta Ceramcoat® glass and acrylic paint · Plaid Treasure Gold finish · Krylon® Make it Stone · Pigma Micron #05 pen.*

INSTRUCTIONS

1 Sand wood for base. Paint bottom and sides gray. Let dry.

2 Turn small cup upside down and put small jar ring on it. The bottom of the cup will become the top of the lighthouse. Use marker to draw a line around cup using top of ring as a guide. Paint cup with Glo Up from rim of cup to line. **Hint:** *Put one hand inside cup to hold it.* Paint with long, even strokes with a lot of paint on brush. Make sure entire cup is covered with paint. When dry, paint a second coat.

3 The "rocks" on large cup, are globs of hot glue. Start at base and work around. Draw outline of rock with glue then fill in center. On next row, center rocks over spaces between rocks on first row.

Paint rocks and area between them black. Paint edge of lid black. Let dry.

Squeeze craft glue along line drawn around smaller cup. Put small jar ring back on cup into the glue. Let dry.

4 Cut a 2½" circle in center of paper. To mask rest of cup, put paper over small jar ring. Apply stone finish to top of cup following manufacturer's directions.

LIGHTING PLAN . . .

A flashlight or electric candle can be put in lower part of lighthouse. Cut a hole in top of large cup to let light shine into small cup.

Electric candle will either have a switch on cord or can be unplugged.

To reach flashlight switch, cut a small hole in side of large cup. Tape flashlight in place so switch stays by the hole. If you don't want to cut a hole in lighthouse, remove large cup to turn switch on and off.

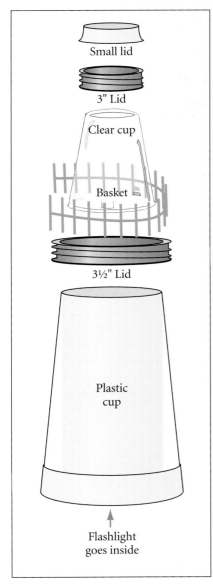

Small lid

3" Lid

Clear cup

Basket

3½" Lid

Plastic cup

Flashlight goes inside

"You are the light of the world" Matthew 5:13

With lid on large cup, put stone finish on cup and lid. Before "stone" dries remove finish between rocks with cotton swabs so black paint will show. Let dry.

5 For lighthouse railing, cut strips from middle of berry basket, 1½" from top of basket. Cut enough strips to measure 10½". Hot glue pieces together so railing fits in large jar ring. When railing is long enough, rub gold finish on it with soft cloth. Glue ends to make a circle.

6 For sandy beach, cut sandpaper same size as top of base. Glue sandpaper on base. Glue felt circles on bottom corners of base. Glue large lid on center of base.

7 Copy verse onto paper. Rub pencil over back of words until completely covered. With letters facing, tape words on base. Trace over letters with sharp pencil. Remove paper and trace over letters with marker. Go over large words twice to make lettering bolder. *Note: Word strip could be generated by computer, cut out, and decoupaged on base.*

8 Turn large cup so bottom becomes top. Hot glue large jar ring, rim up, on top of cup. Set railing in ring. Put a line of hot glue on top of large cup where small cup will set. Quickly set small cup in place. Glue rocks and dried moss around base of lighthouse. ■

by Kari Lee

Lace together long-lasting leather boxes.

MATERIALS FOR RED BOX

- ▶ 6¾" hexagon hat box
- ▶ Two 8½"x11" suede trim pieces
- ▶ One 2-yard hank of gold suede lace
- ▶ One 2-yard hank of blue suede lace

MATERIALS FOR BLUE BOX

- ▶ 7½" hexagon hat box
- ▶ Two 8½"x11" suede trim pieces
- ▶ One 2-yard hank of suede lace in each color: gold, orange, purple, red

MATERIALS FOR BOTH

- ▶ Leather punches*
- ▶ Mallet*
- ▶ Cutting board*
- ▶ Leathercraft cement*
- ▶ Leather shears*
- ▶ Red & blue acrylic paint
- ▶ Poster board
- ▶ Black fine-tip marker
- ▶ Two 1" brushes (one to apply paint and one to apply cement)
- ▶ Pencil, ruler

* The following products from The Leather Factory were used for this project: Maxi punch set, poly mallet, poly cutting board, Tanners Bond® Leathercraft Cement, leathercraft shears.

INSTRUCTIONS

1 For template, place lid on box. Draw a pencil line just below lip of lid on box. Number each panel around base of the box 1 through 6.

To make sure suede panels will fit properly, measure length of each panel 1 through 5, and select average length.

2 Remove lid and measure height of box panel from pencil line, down to bottom of box. Cut out a poster board template using height and length measurements.

Mark the position of holes on template. For red box, place each hole ⅜" from edge and ⅜" apart. For blue box, place each hole ⅜" from edge and ½" apart.

3 Paint inside and outside edge of lid and around top edge of box.

For box base, apply paint along each corner and out about ½". Paint the inside and around top outside lip, past pencil guide lines.

Paint bottom of box with two coats to give a finished look. Let paint dry between coats.

Having the right tools for working with leather makes it a lot easier and more fun!

4 Cut suede pieces. Lay panel template on top side of suede and trace six times with marker. Use leather shears to cut out panels, cutting just inside the lines.

Position template on each suede panel to mark the position of holes. Punch holes using a #7 or $^{13}/_{64}$" tube punch.

Place lid of box upside down on suede and trace with marker. Cut out suede just inside the lines.

5 Glue on suede. Apply a thin coat of cement to top piece on box lid. Cut lengths of colored lace for edge trim. Place a bead of cement along backside of lace length and press into place.

Apply a thin coat of cement on back and center of suede panels. Make sure not to get cement closer than $^{1}/_{4}$" from holes. Press panels onto side of box.

6 Lace panels together using a double whip stitch. For red box, cut six 8" lengths of gold and six 8" lengths of blue lace for outside corners.

For blue box, cut six 12" lengths of gold and two 12" lengths of red, purple, and orange lace for outside corners.

Select a color of lace. Begin to whip stitch from inside of first hole on left at top of a suede panel, leaving a 1" tail of lace. Cross lace over and through second hole from top of adjoining panel on right. Thread lace out second hole opposite, on left. Keep lace very loose.

Select second color of lace. Begin to whip stitch as before but from hole on right. Cross lace over other lace and through same hole other lace is exiting. Thread lace out second hole opposite on right.

Slowly begin to pull stitches snug, with same tension. Make sure lace is not twisted for best appearance. Continue to whip stitch down suede panel.

Cut off all excess lace ends just under suede trim. Apply a small dab of cement on underside of suede and press to hold.

Repeat these steps on remaining five corners. ■

DANIEL & THE LION

by Cindy Groom Harry® and Staff

MATERIALS

▶ Adjustable air freshener*
▶ 2½" plastic foam ball
▶ Acrylic paint*: Flesh Tone, Lamp Black, White Wash, Santa Red, Baby Pink, Sable Brown, Baby Blue
▶ 12"x22" piece purple fabric
▶ 72" length of ¼" metallic gold rickrack
▶ 2" square Antique White felt*
▶ 30" yellow cord
▶ Chenille stems
· Purple: two 5" jumbo, one 12" regular
· Gold: two 12" jumbo, one 5" regular
▶ Pom poms: two 2" gold, one ½" gold, three ¾" gold; one ¼" light brown
▶ Two 10mm wiggle eyes
▶ 9" length of gold jumbo loopy chenille
▶ 6" length black whiskers*
▶ Serrated knife
▶ Small and medium paint-brushes*
▶ Glue gun and glue sticks*
▶ Thick craft glue
▶ Fine sandpaper, graphite paper, pencil, ruler, scissors, ¾"-wide masking tape, wire cutter.

* The following products were used for this project: Dial Renuzit® Long Last™ Adjustable Air Freshener* · DecoArt™ Americana™ acrylic paint · Kunin Felt/Foss Rainbow™ Felt · One & Only Creations® Animal Whiskers™ · Adhesive Technologies Crafty® Multitemp® glue gun and Magic Melt® glue sticks · Loew-Cornell® paintbrushes.

INSTRUCTIONS

☺ Adult supervision needed when working with glue gun and knife.
☺ Trace and cut out pattern.

DANIEL

1 For head, use serrated knife to cut a slice off bottom of foam ball. Lightly sand edges of slice. Use glue gun to attach flat edge of ball on top of air freshener. Paint head with two coats Flesh Tone. Let dry. See Figure 1. Transfer face to head. Paint eyes black, blue, and white. Paint eyebrows black. Paint mouth red. Paint nose brown. Paint cheeks pink.

2 For sleeve, cut 3½" fabric square. Cut a 3½" strip of masking tape.

See Figure 2. Put tape along one edge of wrong side of square covering one half the width of tape. Roll fabric into a cylinder with tape on inside, sticking opposite side of square on remaining half of tape. See Figure 3. Tape sleeve to side of air freshener, just below head. Repeat for other sleeve.

3 For coat, cut 10½" fabric square. See Figure 4. Roll fabric into a cylinder with wrong side out. Center a 6" strip of masking tape on inside of bottom half of front seam. See Figure 5. Place coat over air freshener with taped seam at center front. Wrap a regular purple chenille stem around neck and twist in back, making sure

sleeves are above stem. Use wire cutter to trim ends. See Figure 6. Pull top coat and sleeves down over stem, adjusting gathers at neckline. Fold under ¼" along both center front edges of coat and glue down.

Face

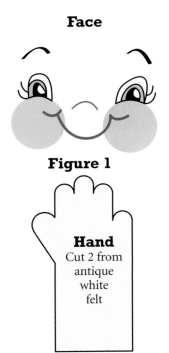

Figure 1

Hand
Cut 2 from
antique
white
felt

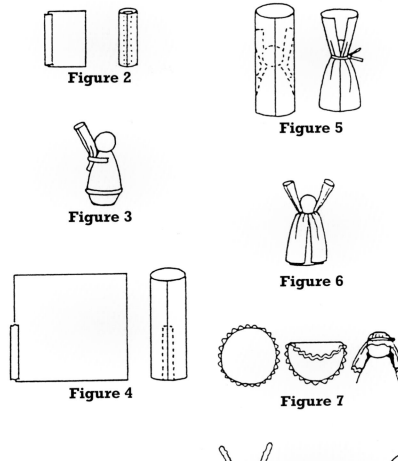

Figure 2

Figure 3

Figure 4

Figure 5

Figure 6

Figure 7

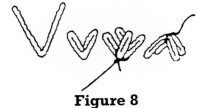

Figure 8

Wrap 6½" length of rickrack around neck. Glue ends. Repeat for 8" length of rickrack. Glue rickrack down on front of robe. Glue remaining rickrack along edges of sleeves and both hems, cutting lengths as needed.

4 Glue hands inside sleeves with thumbs pointing toward front. Cut two 5" lengths purple jumbo chenille stems. Fold each in half. Insert one in each sleeve, gluing ends at shoulder.

5 For headdress, cut a 7" diameter fabric circle. See Figure 7. Glue remaining rickrack around outside edge. Fold under 2½" for center front. Glue on top of head. For headband, glue 11" length of yellow cord around head, knotting at side.

6 For belt, glue 18" yellow cord around waist and knot.

LION

1 For body, glue two 2" pom poms together.
For mane, glue 9" length of loopy chenille around head pom pom.

2 For jowls, glue two ¾" pom poms on center of face. For mouth, glue ¾" pom pom under jowls. For nose, glue ¼" light brown pom pom on top of jowls. Glue wiggle eyes on face above jowls. Cut six 1" pieces of whiskers. Glue three in each jowl.

3 For legs and tail, cut two 10" lengths gold jumbo chenille stem. Set aside remaining pieces for ears. See Figure 8. Fold each in half and fold ends toward center. For tail, wrap end of slim chenille stem around both centers of legs. Glue on bottom of body. Bend two legs forward and two legs toward sides, making another bend at knee and turning toward front. Glue ½" gold pom pom on end of tail. Shape tail as desired. Glue lion next to Daniel.

4 For ears, cut two 1½" lengths gold jumbo chenille stem. Fold each in half and glue cut ends between mane and head pom pom. ∎

TO REFRESHEN GEL

Replace original air-freshener gel when it is depleted with a new container base. If project base is decorated, remove dried gel. From new container, remove new, non-toxic gel. Slip it over post of decorated base and reposition decorated topper.

For FREE Renuzit® Adjustable Air Freshener Craft Project sheets, send $1 for postage and handling and a long self-addressed envelope to: Renuzit® Crafts, Cindy Groom Harry, 2363 - 460th St., Dept. K DANIEL, Ireton, IA 51027.

PUPPY PICTURE FRAME

by Annabelle Keller

MATERIALS
- Photograph
- 8"x8"x½" plastic foam*
- White and black acrylic paint*
- Exterior/interior matte varnish
- Paintbrushes*: #5 round, 1" wash
- 3"x5" white cardstock
- Two ¼" black round buttons
- 15mm animal nose
- Serrated knife
- Candle stub or paraffin
- Glue stick
- Thick craft glue*
- Scissors, tracing paper, paper plate, pencil, wax paper, wire cutters, yardstick

* The following products were used for this project: Styrofoam® plastic foam · Velverette® glue · Delta Ceramcoat® acrylic paint and varnish · Loew-Cornell American Painter® paint-brushes.

INSTRUCTIONS
- ☺ Adult supervision is needed when working with serrated knife.
- ☺ Trace and cut out patterns. Follow directions.
- ☺ Let paint dry completely after each coat.

1 Rub candle stub or paraffin on knife. Use knife to cut foam pieces. Use a scrap of foam to gently sand any rough edges.

2 Pour a puddle of white paint on paper plate. Paint all pieces except tail with 2 coats. Pour black paint on paper plate. Paint tail, ears, paw

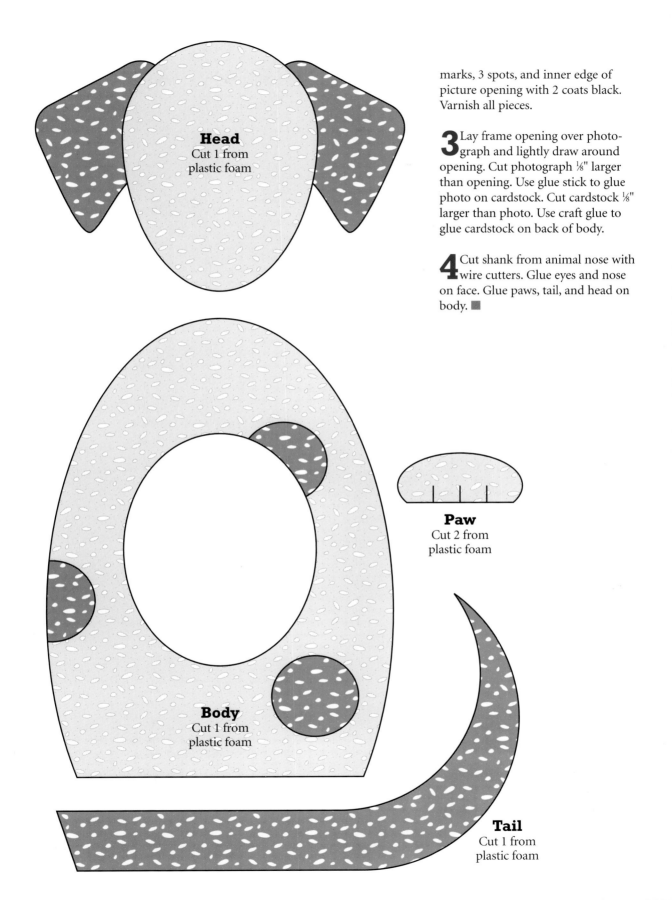

Head
Cut 1 from
plastic foam

marks, 3 spots, and inner edge of
picture opening with 2 coats black.
Varnish all pieces.

3 Lay frame opening over photograph and lightly draw around
opening. Cut photograph ⅛" larger
than opening. Use glue stick to glue
photo on cardstock. Cut cardstock ⅛"
larger than photo. Use craft glue to
glue cardstock on back of body.

4 Cut shank from animal nose with
wire cutters. Glue eyes and nose
on face. Glue paws, tail, and head on
body. ■

Paw
Cut 2 from
plastic foam

Body
Cut 1 from
plastic foam

Tail
Cut 1 from
plastic foam

PICKET FENCE FRAME

by Julie McGuffee

MATERIALS

- ▶ Cherry wood stain marker*
- ▶ Chisel tip markers*: Country Blue, Carnation, Arctic White, Yellow, Pumpkin, Violet, Forest Green, Crimson, Burnt Umber
- ▶ 03 black wood marker*
- ▶ Wood pieces*
  - · Picket fence frame
  - · 3¼"x4½" rectangle
  - · Four ½" birch button plugs
  - · Five ¾" circles
  - · Mini bird
- ▶ Wood craft shapes*: 24 small teardrops, 3 small hexagons, 2 large teardrops, 2 medium teardrops, 2 small teardrops
- ▶ Thick craft glue
- ▶ Few strands of raffia

* The following products were used for this project: ZIG® Woodcraft® Stain, Chisel Tip, and wood markers · Lara's Crafts wood parts · Forster® Woodsies™ wood craft shapes.

INSTRUCTIONS

1 Stain picket fence frame with stain marker. Paint small wood pieces as follows: 8 small teardrops - Country Blue; 8 small teardrops - Violet; 8 small teardrops - Carnation; Remaining teardrops - Forest Green; Mini bird - Crimson, with yellow beak; 3 small hexagons - Yellow, outlined with Pumpkin.

2 See photo. Draw outline edges of frame and lines for boards on front of frame with chisel edge of Burnt Umber marker. Draw lines and ovals with black marker to look like wood grain. Draw spirals in flower petals with black marker.

3 Glue teardrop petals on back of hexagons to make 3 flowers. Glue 2 circles together twice and glue on back of Country Blue and Violet flowers for spacers so flowers stand out on frame. Glue one circle on back of Carnation flower.

4 See photo. Glue flowers on front of frame. Glue leaves on frame under flowers. Add white dots on flower centers, using tip of paintbrush dipped in paint. Paint a few 3-dot clusters around flowers. Glue wire on top of frame or make a small hole in each corner and thread wire through from back to front. Curl ends of wire around paintbrush handle. Hold 6 strands of raffia together and tie in a bow around wire. Glue bird on center of bow. Use black marker to make a dot for eye, small speckles, and a line for wing.

5 Hold rectangle on back of frame over opening. Glue a button plug on each corner. (Rectangle is held in place by lip of plug.) Position photo behind opening and slide rectangle in place to hold photo securely. ■

SEASHORE CANISTER SET

by Shelia Sommers

MATERIALS

- ▶ Glass canisters
- ▶ Glass paint*: Maize, Burnt Sienna, Cotton Candy Pink, Red-Red, Ultra Black, Ultra White, Light Blue, Cobalt Blue
- ▶ Surface conditioner*
- ▶ Clear gloss glaze*
- ▶ #1 wash paintbrush
- ▶ Nautical stencil with border*
- ▶ Stencil sponge
- ▶ Cotton swabs, dishwashing soap, lint-free towel

* Delta PermEnamel® glass, tile and ceramic paint, surface conditioner, gloss glaze, Cherished Memories nautical stencil and stencil sponge were used for this project.

INSTRUCTIONS

1 Wash canisters with soap and water. Dry with lint-free towel. Follow manufacturer's directions to apply surface conditioner.

Wash hands before beginning to paint. Dirt and oils found naturally on skin will keep paint from sticking on glass.

2 Paint wide Cobalt Blue band around bottom of each canister. See photo. Stencil separate designs randomly on canisters, using stencil sponge and following colors: Red-Red - thin bands around lighthouse, bottom of sailboat; Ultra White - wide bands around lighthouse, sail on sailboat; Ultra Black - seagulls, lighthouse roof; Burnt Sienna - sailboat mast; Maize - starfish, sand beneath lighthouse; Cotton Candy Pink - fan shell; Light Blue - Conch shell. Sponge sailboat flags with color of your choice.

Dip cotton swab in White and paint dot clouds.

3 Position anchor border around edge of lid and sponge on Cobalt Blue. Continue color up over edge onto top of lid. Sponge Maize rope design.

4 Position large anchor design on top of lid and sponge black. When all paint is dry, apply a coat of gloss glaze to all painted areas.

5 Don't use or wash canisters for 10 days while paint cures. After 10 days they will be dishwasher safe. ■

MOSAIC FISH TREASURE BOX

by Susan Lowenthal

INSTRUCTIONS

☺ Trace and cut out patterns. Follow directions.

1 Make two copies of the pattern. Tape one copy under lid.

2 Pick pieces of glass that fit onto the second pattern. This pattern will act as model. Start with fish and work out towards edge of pattern.

3 "Paint" glue on box top. Work only a small area at a time. Start with fish eye, then face, fin, and tail. Pick up pieces of glass from second pattern and glue on box top in the same position. Use fingers or tweezers. Let glue set up for about 15-20 minutes.

4 Outline head, fin, and tail with leading. Let dry 15 minutes. Do body in the same way. Outline whole fish with leading. For heavier line, wait a few minutes and outline again.

6 Follow the same steps for seaweed and coral. Let dry one hour.

7 When dry, glue the water and fish bubbles on box in the same way. Work from fish out toward edges. Let dry overnight. ■

MATERIALS

▶ Plastic or acrylic box
▶ Art glass: yellow, clear, green, red, blue, sapphire, amethyst*
▶ Jewelry glue*
▶ Liquid leading*
▶ Masking tape
▶ Tweezers
▶ Pencil, scissors, tracing paper, scissors, tweezers

The following products were used for this project: Optimum Art Glass Cobbles · Beacon Adhesives Fabri-Tac Glue · Plaid Gallery Glass Liquid Leading.

Adjust size of pattern to fit top of box.

BUTTERFLY NECKLACE & BARRETTE

by Susan Lowenthal

Butterfly Necklace
Cut 1 from clear plastic

MATERIALS FOR BOTH

- ▶ Art Glass*
  - · Yellow and red
  - · Minis - mixed colors
- ▶ Sheet of clear plastic*
- ▶ Thin blue wire*
- ▶ Necklace Clasp
- ▶ Barrette
- ▶ Hole punch
- ▶ Jewelry glue*
- ▶ Beads of your choice
- ▶ Paper plates, tracing paper, pencil, scissors, tweezers

* The following products were used for this project: Cobbles from Optimum Art Glass Company · Cobbles Canvas (sheet of plastic) · Refill pack of wire from Wire Art · Fabri-Tac Glue from Beacon Adhesives.

INSTRUCTIONS

☺ Trace and cut out patterns. Follow directions.

1 Pull off paper from both sides of plastic butterflies. Punch a hole through each wing of necklace butterfly. Do not cover holes with glass.

2 Place butterfly on paper plate to catch glass as it is sprinkled. Apply glue all over butterfly. For body, place red pieces in middle of butterfly. Sprinkle different colors of mini cobbles on wings. Gently pat glass in place. Let butterfly dry overnight.

3 For necklace, cut two 3" lengths of wire. Place wires through holes in wings and twist together. String beads, then twist a loop in wire for fastening

next section. Wrap wire around pencil to form coils. Fold wire to hold beads in place. Continue until necklace is completed. Finish last bead connector by looping it through a clasp.

4 Glue butterfly on barrette. Glue glass on each side of barrette. ■

Barrette
Cut 1 from clear plastic

THE WORLD OF WINDMILLS
A Learning Skit

by Bill Stephani

Krista, Alex, Jacob, and Garrett are cousins and often walk home from school together. On their way home today, Krista is explaining her problem.

Krista: Geez! I don't know how I'll ever get my report done by next week.

Garrett: How long have you known about it?

Krista: Oh, about four months. But now I'm running out of time and need to get it done!

Jacob: What are you writing about?

Krista: I think windmills are cool, so I'm doing my report on Dutch windmills. But I don't know where to start.

Garrett: Why don't we go ask Papa about them. He told me he went to Holland once, and he read a bunch of books about all kinds of windmills.

Krista: I should have remembered that!

They knock on Papa's door.

Krista *(Bursting with excitement)*: Papa, I need your help! Can you tell me all about windmills?

Papa: Whoa, slow down! You're creating some wind yourself.

Alex: Where does the wind come from anyway?

Papa: Oh, you can blame the sun for that. The sun warms the earth unevenly, and when warm air expands and rises, cold air rushes in and takes its place. We call this air

Thousands of wind turbins generate electricity across the U.S. and Canada.

Not only is the wind free, but it is clean and safe for all of us.

movement the wind. Can you think of ways the wind helps us?

Jacob: It's sure easier riding my bike when the wind is on my back.

Garrett: It makes my kite fly, and it helps airplanes stay up.

Krista: The wind pushes sailboats across the water. Columbus couldn't have discovered America without the wind.

Papa: And it also makes windmills work.

Garrett: What are windmills for, Papa?

Papa: Oh, they're for many things. Until the year 1900, they were the most powerful machines in the world. The wind turned sails that were connected to shafts and gears. Windmills ground grain for flour and pumped water to drain swamps or to irrigate crops. They made oil for lamps, sawed lumber, made paper and paint, ground cocoa, gunpowder, malt, and mustard. Windmills even made arsenic poison.

Jacob: Why would they want to make poison?

Papa: Arsenic is a dangerous poison, but it was also used to make insecticides, glass, and medicines. Now it's even used to preserve wood.

Krista: Oh, I've seen that green wood they use outside.

Papa: Years ago, some mills ground cow hides and animal bones into glue. When I was going to grade school, some of the kids used to eat glue while we worked on projects.

Alex: Oh yuk! They must not have known what it was made of.

Papa: Worse than glue-making mills, they had mills called "fulling mills" that pounded woolen cloth into felt. The Dutch called these "stink mills" because rotten butter and old urine were used in the process.

Krista: That's disgusting!

Alex: How did they do all this work before windmills were invented?

Papa: In the olden days, men or animals turned heavy millstones by walking around and around in a circle pushing a log that turned heavy stones that slid together to grind materials. They did it hour after hour and day after day.

Jacob: That sounds like terrible work. I guess I won't complain anymore about taking out the garbage.

Garrett: How big were windmills?

Papa: They came in all sizes. Sawmills could stand 80 feet high! They contained hoists, gears, and saws. Their sails could be 100 feet across.

Jacob: Did they make small ones, too?

Papa: Some farms had small windmills to pump water that stood only five feet tall.

Alex: How many kinds of windmills are there anyway?

Papa: Lots. They came in all kinds of shapes just like grandkids! Some of the oldest were something like our

revolving doors. They were covered on two sides, and the wind turned them as it blew through.

Garrett: I saw some windmills that look like giant airplane propellers. What are they for?

Papa: Those are called wind turbins, and they generate electricity.

Alex: Our teacher told us that a bunch of wind turbins together are called wind farms. She also said that there are thousands across the U.S. and Canada.

Garrett: Don't windmills pump water, too?

Papa: At one time there were six million windmills pumping water on the dry western plains.

Krista: Why aren't there that many anymore?

Papa: Now they use electric and gasoline power instead of the wind.

Garrett: But wouldn't the wind be a lot cheaper? Isn't the wind free?

Papa: Not only is it free, but it's also clean and safe for all of us to use.

Krista: I'm interested in the Dutch windmills. Aren't they the ones we usually see in pictures?

Papa: I think Dutch windmills are the most popular, and they're the ones we think of when we think of windmills. The Dutch had windmills way back in 1600. They used windmills to pump water out of lakes and marshes. Then they built dikes to hold the water back.

Jacob: Where do the Dutch live?

Papa: They live in the Netherlands which means low lands. Much of the country is near or below sea level.

Alex: I wonder what it was like for a person running a windmill.

Papa: It must have been a hard life. When the wind blew hard, a miller worked for days without stopping. During a storm, he had to make sure the mill made it through safely.

Alex: Where did millers live? Did they live right in the windmill?

Papa: It depended on what kind of windmill it was. A miller and his family usually lived next door to a grinding mill. But if it was a drainage windmill, they probably lived right inside the windmill. They had two doors on opposite sides so when the sails were blocking one door, they could use the other door. These drainage windmills were usually isolated and a long way from towns.

Garrett: Wouldn't they get lonely?

Papa: I'm sure they did. But sometimes travelers would pass by and stay for awhile. The children could
Continued on page 57.

DUTCH WINDMILL CUTOUT

By John Michael Cook

GENERAL INSTRUCTIONS

1 Adult help is recommended. Use windmill photo and drawings as guides.

2 Cut out all parts. Score fold lines. Scoring means to make a light groove so folds are straight and neat. A ruler and the tip of a letter opener work well.

3 Tools and materials needed include: scissors, ruler, scoring tool, 4 corn-dog sticks (or ¼" dowels), thick craft glue, 4 square toothpicks, wax paper.

4 For sail supports, cut sharp points off 4 corn-dog sticks, leaving a length of 5¾". For main windmill shaft, cut 1 stick 3½" long. Follow directions on page 55.

5 After pivot cradle is assembled and glued, glue the two short pivots in place as shown. Before the main wind shaft is inserted into the pivot cradle, slide on 2 main wind shaft spacers (from page 53), then the long pivot, then 2 main wind shaft spacers.

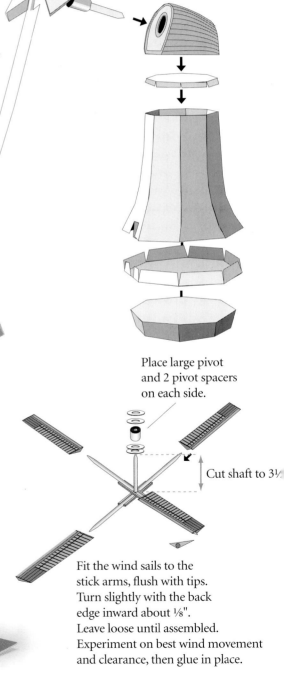

Place large pivot and 2 pivot spacers on each side.

Cut shaft to 3½

Fit the wind sails to the stick arms, flush with tips. Turn slightly with the back edge inward about ⅛". Leave loose until assembled. Experiment on best wind movement and clearance, then glue in place.

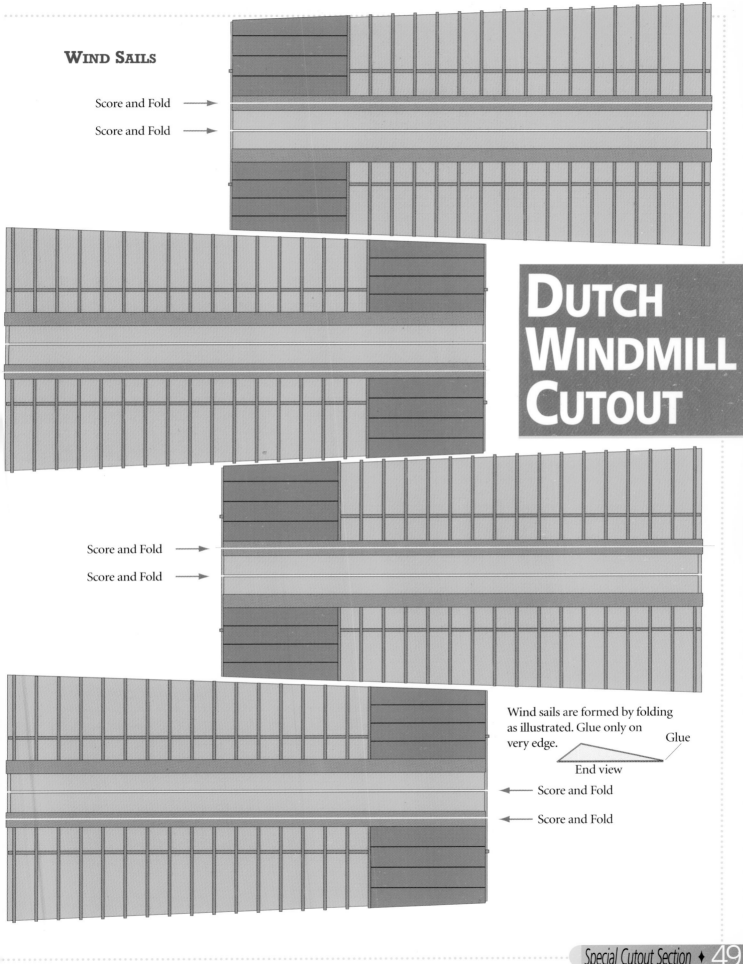

WIND SAILS

Score and Fold

Score and Fold

DUTCH WINDMILL CUTOUT

Score and Fold

Score and Fold

Wind sails are formed by folding as illustrated. Glue only on very edge.

Glue

End view

Score and Fold

Score and Fold

MAIN UPPER BUILDING SEGMENTS

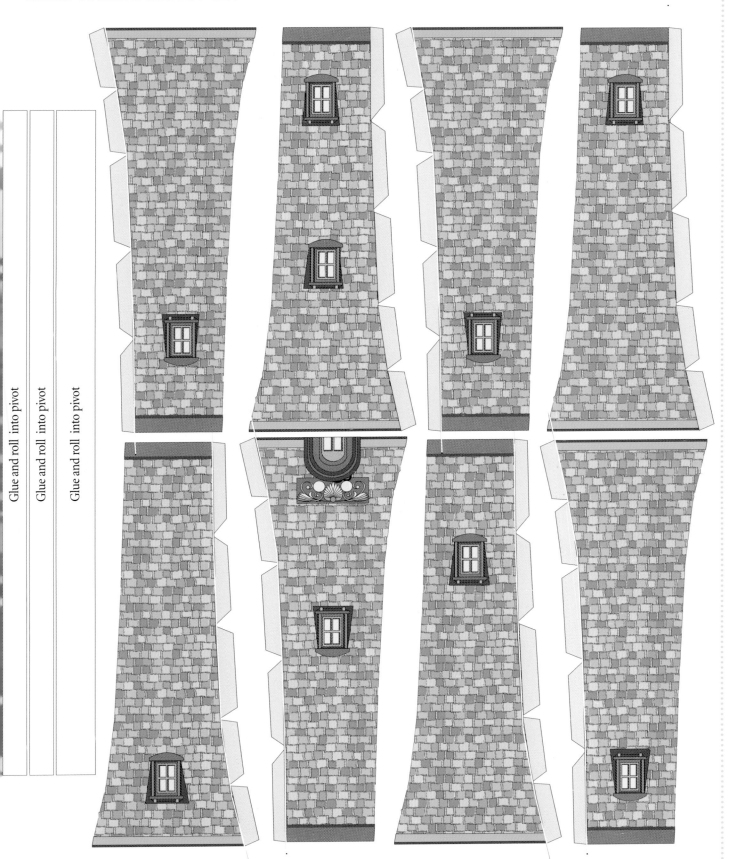

Glue and roll into pivot

Glue and roll into pivot

Glue and roll into pivot

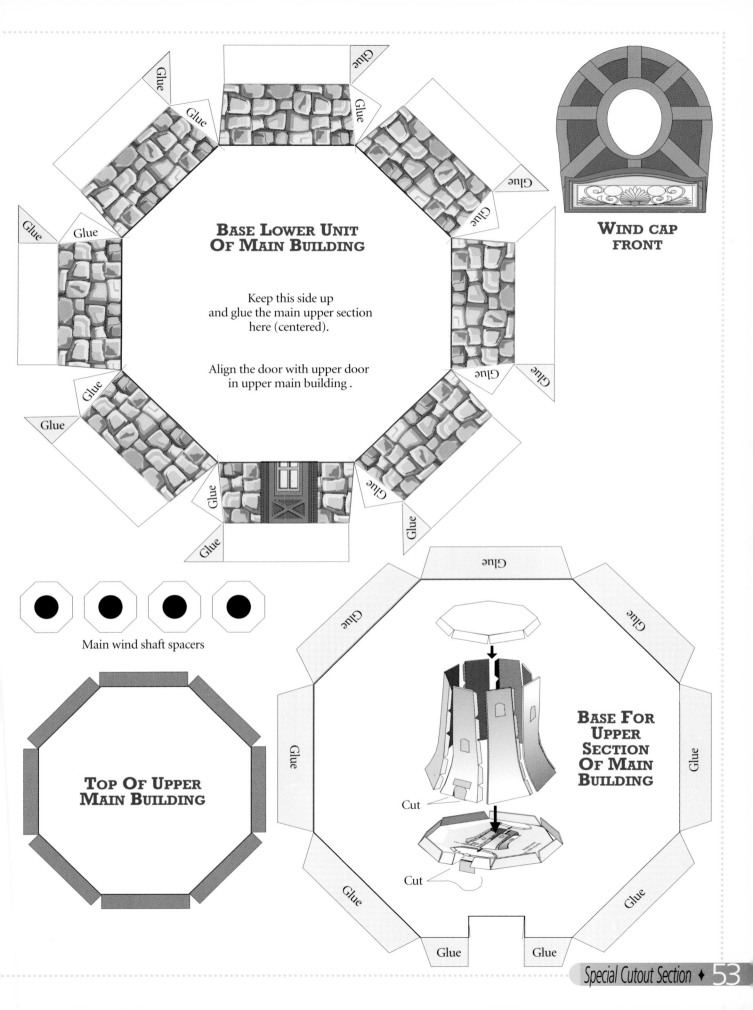

BASE LOWER UNIT OF MAIN BUILDING

Keep this side up
and glue the main upper section
here (centered).

Align the door with upper door
in upper main building .

Glue (multiple tabs around the octagon)

WIND CAP FRONT

Main wind shaft spacers

TOP OF UPPER MAIN BUILDING

BASE FOR UPPER SECTION OF MAIN BUILDING

Cut

Cut

Glue

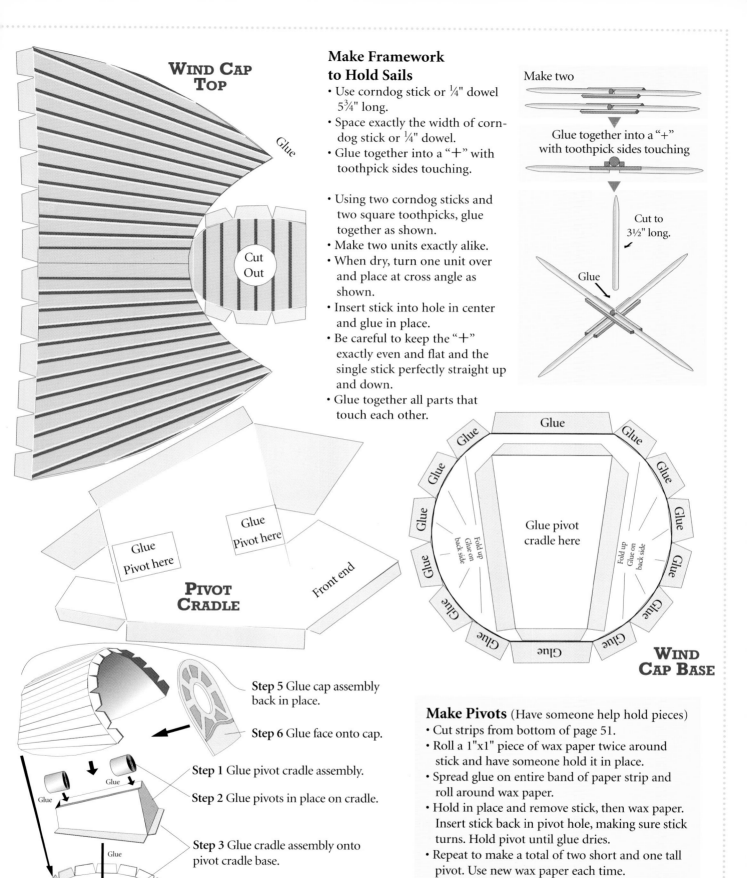

WIND CAP TOP

Glue

Cut Out

Make Framework to Hold Sails

- Use corndog stick or ¼" dowel 5¾" long.
- Space exactly the width of corndog stick or ¼" dowel.
- Glue together into a "+" with toothpick sides touching.

- Using two corndog sticks and two square toothpicks, glue together as shown.
- Make two units exactly alike.
- When dry, turn one unit over and place at cross angle as shown.
- Insert stick into hole in center and glue in place.
- Be careful to keep the "+" exactly even and flat and the single stick perfectly straight up and down.
- Glue together all parts that touch each other.

Make two

Glue together into a "+" with toothpick sides touching

Cut to 3½" long.

Glue

Glue

Glue
Pivot here

Glue
Pivot here

Glue
Pivot here

PIVOT CRADLE

Front end

Glue   Glue   Glue   Glue   Glue
Glue   Glue   Glue   Glue
Glue   Glue   Glue   Glue   Glue
Glue   Glue

Fold up Glue on back side

Glue pivot cradle here

Fold up Glue on back side

WIND CAP BASE

Step 5 Glue cap assembly back in place.

Step 6 Glue face onto cap.

Step 1 Glue pivot cradle assembly.

Glue

Glue

Step 2 Glue pivots in place on cradle.

Step 3 Glue cradle assembly onto pivot cradle base.

Glue

Step 4 Glue mill cap onto pivot base. Start in back and work both sides forward. Keep centered and bottom flat.

Glue   Glue   Glue   Glue

Make Pivots (Have someone help hold pieces)

- Cut strips from bottom of page 51.
- Roll a 1"x1" piece of wax paper twice around stick and have someone hold it in place.
- Spread glue on entire band of paper strip and roll around wax paper.
- Hold in place and remove stick, then wax paper. Insert stick back in pivot hole, making sure stick turns. Hold pivot until glue dries.
- Repeat to make a total of two short and one tall pivot. Use new wax paper each time.

Continued from page 47.

swim and fish in the canals. In winter they would skate on the frozen canals.

Krista: Didn't these guys ever get to go away on vacation?

Papa: Not very often. The wind-millers had to turn the mill or adjust the sails in all kinds of weather. They had to climb 20 feet up to adjust the sails. In bad weather they had to roll the sail part way up so the wind would blow through.

Garrett: I'll bet that was cold work in the winter.

Alex: Especially when the sails froze.

Jacob: I'll bet their fingers froze, too.

Krista: Boy, it sounds like dangerous work.

Papa: There were many dangers besides changing the sails. In grinding mills, millstones had to be covered with grain. Otherwise, the stones grinding together could make sparks and start a fire. Many mills burned to the ground even during rainstorms. Lightning could also strike and set fires that burned the mills.

Krista: Didn't people get hurt?

Papa: Many millers had arms and legs injured by gears that broke or went out of control. Some people were crushed and killed. These wind-mills were also very noisy and millers could go deaf from the grinding and pounding sounds.

Alex: Did other mills smell bad like the fulling mill?

Garrett: Did they smell as bad as a pig farm?

Papa: Besides smelling bad, the fumes could be deadly. A paint

miller, who ground wood for paint dyes, wore a wet sponge over his mouth and nose so he wouldn't breathe the harmful fumes. He had to drink large amounts of milk.

Jacob: Why? Did the work make him thirsty?

Papa: They drank milk to help remove the harmful dust from the stomach before it went into the bloodstream.

Krista: What did they do when the wind wasn't blowing?

Papa: I don't think they had many days off. They had to lubricate the gears and teeth with beeswax. Sometimes they greased parts using old pig's fat. They would hang pieces from the rafters to age -- the older the fat, the better . . . Sometimes it was more than 20 years old.

Garrett: I guess it would smell like a really *old* pig farm.

Krista: How could they tell wind-mills apart?

Papa: The Dutch passed a law in 1693 ordering that all the windmills had to have a name. Some of the names were The Cat, The Seagull, The Iron Hog . . .

Jacob: What did they call the smelly ones?

Krista: How about The Skunk,

Alex: Or The Rotten Apple.

Garrett: Or The Smelly Pig!

Papa: Windmills were very important. They were places to get together and learn the latest news. The grain mills became popular places to buy flour and to get together for the latest gossip. The miller knew weather better than anyone else, so they came to him for forecasts.

Krista: Our teacher said that wind-mills were used as signals, too.

Papa: That's right. For example, sails set in "X" meant the miller was on vacation or the mill was closed for awhile. Streamers or flags were hung from the sails to announce good news like a wedding or birth of a baby. During the war, they signaled when the enemy was coming.

Alex: Wow! Windmills were really important!

Krista: Gee, Papa. I was so interested in what you were saying that I forgot to take notes for my report. Can you start all over again?

Papa: I have an even better idea. Let's all go to the library and see if we can find books that have all this information written down.

Krista: I wish all my reports could be this much fun! Thanks, Papa! ▪

by Moliver Made

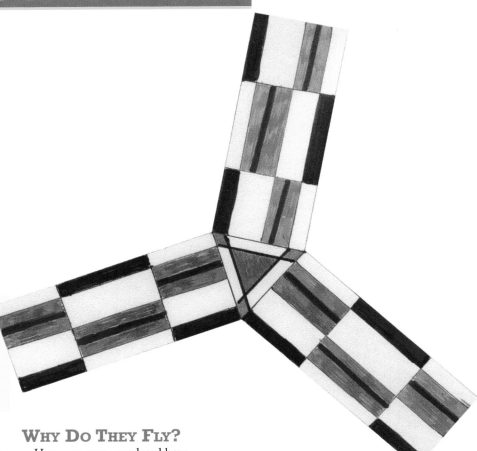

MATERIALS
- 8½"x11" white card stock
- Markers, crayons, or rubber stamps and stamp pad
- Graphite paper, pencil, scissors, tracing paper

INSTRUCTIONS

1 Trace around boomerang on this page. Transfer pattern onto card stock. Cut it out.

2 Decorate with markers, crayons, or use rubber stamps. *Note: Stickers will change the balance and airflow, so they're not recommended. But if you want to experiment, try to place them evenly.*

3 To make paper look like wood, draw knots first. Run lines around them keeping them all going in the same general direction. Every piece of wood looks different and has natural imperfections, so you can't get it wrong.

4 Flip boomerang like a Frisbee and get ready to catch it. With practice it will return to you.

PHOTO 23 (Will need to be 100 per cent because they also serve as patterns)

WHY DO THEY FLY?

Have you ever wondered how things that are heavier than air can fly? You may have thought that bugs and birds only fly because they flap their wings, but this is only partly correct.

There are pictures and stories of flying machines that date back long ago. We can tell from the early mythological story of Icarus that man has tried to fly for a very long time.

EARLY ATTEMPTS

Early attempts to fly imitated the way birds fly by flapping feathered wings. They all failed.

Leonardo Da Vinci, painter of the famous Mona Lisa, sketched helicopters during the 16th century. The sketches never got off the ground, but it got other people thinking.

It wasn't until 1903, at Kitty Hawk, North Carolina, that Orville and Wilbur Wright successfully flew a heavier-than-air flying machine. Of the four flights they flew on December 17, the longest was 59 seconds at 30 miles per hour. In contrast, a modern day fighter jet can now travel at speeds over 2,000 miles per hour. At that speed, it would be traveling 30 miles in a minute.

HOW DO THINGS FLY?

Aerodynamics is the study of air and the forces on an object. We know that when we throw a ball, it arcs through the air and falls in a smooth curve. Why then does a paper plane stay up longer and glide smoothly to the ground? We can rule out weight when compare a big heavy Styrofoam plane and a ping-pong ball.

In fact, a bigger, heavier plane stays in the air longer and flies farther then a paper plane. There are mysterious forces at work here. One force we all know about is gravity. The bigger and heavier the object, the greater the gravitational force.

For example, the sun is so massive that it keeps all the planets revolving around it rather than them spinning off into cold, dark space. Gravity is the force that keeps things grounded, but what force makes things fly?

The flight of planes, boomerangs, and birds is controlled by gravity, lift, drag, and thrust. The opposite of gravity is called lift. You may have noticed that airplane wings are curved on the top and flat on the bottom side. The curved top surface is longer than the flat side.

BERNOULLI'S PRINCIPLE

As the air tries to stay together flowing over the wing it must travel faster over the top curve to catch up with the straight flow on the bottom side.

A man named Bernoulli discovered that the faster the air flow, the lower the air pressure. This is called Bernoulli's law and is the principle that man used to create flying devices. Air pressure, like all types of pressure, is a pushing force.

When the air is moving faster over the top of the wing than under the bottom, it creates a greater air pressure under the wing, pushing the wing (and everything connected to it) upward -- lifting it into the air.

Everything from bugs and birds to helicopters and jumbo jets use this principle to take off and stay airborne.

THE FORCE OF THRUST

We have to propel (as in propeller), or give motion to an object to make it fly. We call that force thrust. When a body is at rest (not moving) it wants to stay at rest. Scientists call that inertia. (Mom called it being lazy.)

Once something is moving it wants to keep moving until it is slowed down by another force. That is momentum. The slowing down force is friction. When we talk about friction in air it is called drag. Drag works against thrust in the same way that gravity works against lift.

Now, let's get back to those flapping

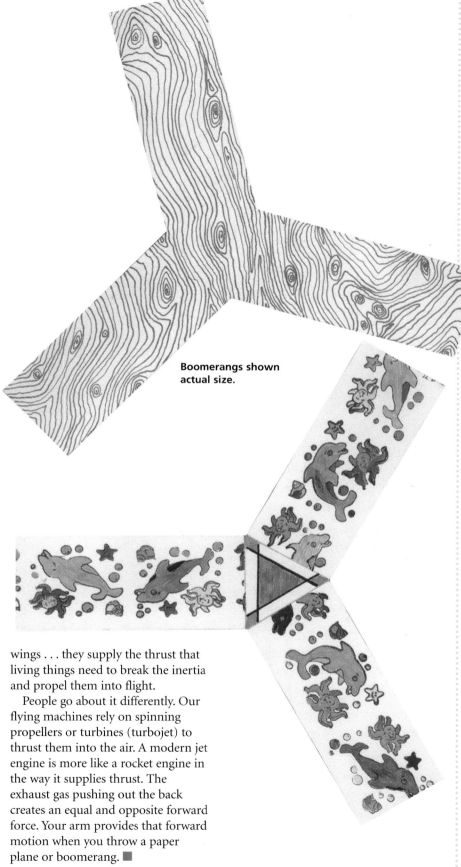

Boomerangs shown actual size.

wings . . . they supply the thrust that living things need to break the inertia and propel them into flight.

People go about it differently. Our flying machines rely on spinning propellers or turbines (turbojet) to thrust them into the air. A modern jet engine is more like a rocket engine in the way it supplies thrust. The exhaust gas pushing out the back creates an equal and opposite forward force. Your arm provides that forward motion when you throw a paper plane or boomerang. ■

MAKE YOUR OWN HYGROMETER

Chenille Stem

Hair

Toothpick

Use a glass cup or jar to watch the daily change in atmosphere

As a storm approaches, humidity in the air increases. When good weather is on the way, humidity decreases. Early American farmers noticed that increased moisture in the air caused a rope to twist tighter. They used this information to build a weather-forecasting device.

They hung a length of hemp rope from a rafter in the barn. Then they tied a heavy wood pointer on the end of the rope just above the floor. When good weather came, the farmer made a mark on the floor where the pointer pointed. When bad weather came, he made a second mark. The farmer could now predict changes in weather when he saw the pointer moving either toward the good-weather mark or the bad-weather mark.

You can make your own hygrometer using the same idea.

INSTRUCTIONS

1 Color the ends of a toothpick 2 different colors. Wrap one end of a single strand of hair around the center of toothpick. Put a drop of glue on the hair to hold it in place.

2 Place chenille stem across the center of the open end of the jar. Bend ends of chenille stem over jar to hold in place. Hang hair strand inside the jar with the toothpick just above the bottom of the jar. Wrap the loose end of the hair around stem and secure it with a drop of glue.

3 Over a period of time, observe the weather. When the weather is good, make a mark on the jar where the toothpick points. When it is rainy or stormy, make a second mark. Write "Rain" and "Clear" where you've

MATERIALS
► Strand of human hair (blonde is best)
► Round toothpick
► Chenille stem
► Wide-mouthed jar
► Glue
► Colored permanent markers

made your marks. Decorate your hygrometer. As your toothpick indicator turns, you should be able to predict changes in weather. ■

JACKS

Bounce the ball and pick up the jacks. It's fun and challenging!

SPIDER TRAP:

Setup with the jacks in between the fingers.

Bounce the ball and swiftly move the jacks between the fingers into the arch of hand.

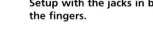

The basic game of Jacks is played by bouncing the ball once and picking up a certain number of jacks before catching the ball -- all with the same hand!

First, toss out the jacks on a flat surface, like you would throw dice. The trick is to not get the jacks too close or too far from each other.

For your first turn use the SAME hand to
• bounce the ball
• pick up one jack
• catch the ball before it bounces twice
Repeat these steps until you have all of the jacks picked up. If you miss, start over again.

For your second turn, pick up two jacks at a time. Then pick up three jacks at a time and so on. As you group the jacks, you will have an odd number of jacks to pick up with the last bounce of each turn.

Continue until you pick up all of the jacks with your last turn. Then you win!

VARIATIONS

The Challenge: As you get more skilled, go back to the beginning anytime you miss.

Competition: To play Jacks with two or more players, sit in a circle. Take turns clockwise. Each player picks up ONE number of jacks in one turn. If they miss, they try to pick up the same number on their next turn until they are successful. The first one to pick up all of the jacks with one bounce wins.

Double Bounce: Let the ball bounce twice before catching it.

Spider Trap: See above photos. Arch your hand. Arrange four jacks between fingers. Instead of picking up the jacks, use the forefinger of your other hand to flick the jacks into the arch of your hand. First flick jacks inside your hand one at a time, then two at a time, and so on. When you flick all four inside your hand with one bounce of the ball you win.

Flip Trick: Lay all of the jacks on the back of your hand. Toss them in the air and try to catch all of them in the palm of your hand.

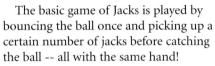

OREGON LOG TRUCK

by Don Messerle

Truck body

Truck bed

Truck bunk

Trailer reach

Trailer bunk

Trailer bed

MATERIALS

- 1"x4"x16" board (bed of truck & trailer)
- 4"x4"x5" board (body)
- Two ½"x¾"x5½" boards (bunks for truck & trailer)
- 32" length of ⅜" wooden dowel (bunk stakes, exhaust pipe, trailer reach)
- ⅛"x¾"x 4¼ board (front bumper).
- Eighteen 1½" purchased wheels
  Option: Wheels can be cut from ⅜" plywood using 1½" circle saw.
- Two 1" wooden half rounds (headlights)
- Two ¾" wooden half rounds (taillights)
- Seven to nine 18" hardwood logs ¾" to 1½" in diameter (dowels could be used)
- Acrylic paint*: red, yellow, black, white, gray
- Paintbrushes: flat and liner
- 1" finishing nails
- 10 staples ¼" wide and ½" long
- Four bolts ¼"x6"
- One bolt ¼"x5"
- Five ¼" nuts
- Thirty two ¼" washers
- Six 1½" wood screws
- Screw eyes: One ¼", two ¾"
- ½" screw hook
- Spray varnish*
- Tools: Band saw or jig saw, screwdriver, hammer, drill and bits, hacksaw
- Two ¼"x18" chains (for binding logs)
- Wood glue*

* The following products were used for this project: Delta® acrylic paints · Beacon™ Fabri-Tac™ Permanent Adhesive · Krylon spray varnish.

With a little help from Dad or Grandpa, you can begin your logging business!

What a great project for Dad and the kids. This truck is made to scale from a working log truck. The scale is ½ inch equals 1 foot.

Use any softwood for all wood in the construction. If you substitute commercial wheels for the home-made wheels, you may eliminate the wheel-making procedure and the use of the drill press and circle saw.

Use hardwood logs on the truck because there is no pitch. The truck pictured has been played with for three years!

INSTRUCTIONS

1 Cut 1"x4" board into a 12" piece for truck bed and one 4" piece for trailer bed. Set aside.

2 See Figure 1. Cut 4"x4" into truck body.

3 Cut ½"x¼"x11" board in half for the two bunks.

Cut dowel into four 3" pieces for bunk stakes, one 15" piece for trailer reach, one 4½" piece for exhaust pipe.

For wheels, drill ¼" in center of all.

Sand all wooden pieces.

4 For truck bunk, use ⅜" bit to drill a ¼" deep hole ⅜" from both ends.

In center of bunk drill a ³⁄₁₆" hole. Countersink center hole. Glue a 3" dowel into each outside hole. Repeat with bunk for trailer.

5 See photo. Paint all pieces appropriate color. Let paint dry.

6 To assemble log truck, attach body of truck to bed of truck with four 1½" wood screws from under the bed. The front of the body should line up with front of bed.

7 To assemble log truck front axle, take a 5" bolt and add a washer, wheel, washer and then washer, wheel, washer and nut. Be sure wheels turn freely. Center axle on underbody 1" from truck front. Attach loosely in two places to body with

Bunk

Bed

Trailer bunk attached to bed

Wheels

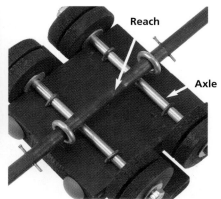

Reach

Axle

Undercarriage of trailer

staples. Tighten nut until both wheels turn freely. Finish pounding staples. Cut off excess bolt with hacksaw. Hit end of bolt with hammer to flatten and remove sharp edges.

For back axles, repeat same process using 6" bolts and adding an additional wheel and washer on each side. Measure from back of body 1¾" and 3¼" to place rear axles.

8 Nail front bumper on truck front. Glue on headlights.

9 Drill a hole for wood screw 2¾" from back of truck body. Screw bunk to body with 1½" wood screw. Place two ¼" washers between bunk and truck body. Tighten screw so bunk turns freely.

10 Nail exhaust pipe vertically ⅜" from back right side of truck body. Attach ½" screw hook to center back bottom edge of truck body.

11 *Optional: Paint detail work around truck windows and paint name of log truck company on the truck door.*

12 Assemble trailer wheels same as for truck in step 7, but place back axles 1" from front and back of trailer bed.

13 Attach trailer bunk same as truck bunk in step 9, centering in trailer bed.

14 Screw ¾" screw into bottom of trailer bed ½" from front and back. Glue taillights on back of trailer bed.

15 For trailer reach, insert ¼" screw eye into one end of reach. Place reach into ¾" screw eyes on bottom of trailer bed making sure that it slides easily in screw eyes. Drive finishing nail through reach at 1" and 5¾" on opposite end from ¼" screw eye. The finishing nails hold reach within the ¾" screw eyes.

16 Spray varnish on entire truck and trailer to preserve color.

17 Attach the trailer reach to truck screw hook with screw eye in reach. Place logs in truck and trailer bunks. Bend one end of each chain into a hook and wrap chain around logs. ∎

Attach headlights with glue.

Completed log truck.

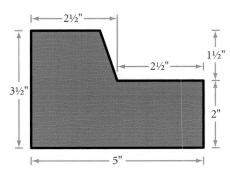

Log Truck Body

Figure 1

2½"

2½"

1½"

3½"

2"

5"

FLOWER POWER DESK SET

by Julie Danielson

The journal has its own ribbon bookmark attached!

Make a matching bookmark for your favorite reading books!

MATERIALS

- Clean empty cans: 11½ ounce, 15¼ ounce
- Pint plastic berry basket
- 12"x18" thick craft foam sheets*: 2 black
- 12"x18" thin craft foam sheets*: 1 each yellow, pink, rose, purple, blue, kelly green
- Paint pens*: Azalea, Soft Blue
- Satin ribbon: 1⅛ yards of ⅛" pink, 1½ yards of 2mm variegated
- 1 blue, 1 pink ½" tinsel pom pom
- 1 pink mini plastic clothespin*
- 65 assorted small buttons
- Large tapestry needle
- Rotary cutter with scallop, wavy, straight blades*
- Paper trimmer*
- 20 sheets 8½"x11" paper
- Thick craft glue
- Measuring tape, paper punch, pencil, ruler, scissors, tracing paper

* The following products were used for this project: Fibre Craft 2mm and 5mm Flexi-Foam craft foam, clothespin, pom poms · ZIG® Large Painty Pens® · Offray ribbon · Fiskars® rotary cutter and blades, paper trimmer.

INSTRUCTIONS

☺ Adult supervision needed when using rotary and paper cutters.

☺ Trace and cut out patterns on page 66. Follow directions.

CUT AND GLUE

1 For bookmark, cut 1½"x6½" thick foam with scallop blade on rotary cutter.

2 For cans, measure around can. Measure height of can. Draw measurements on foam. Cut thin black foam with rotary paper cutter and straight blade. Glue foam around can.

3 For journal, cut a 9"x12" piece of thick black foam. Use rotary cutter and scallop blade to cut piece in half (two 6"x9" pieces). Use hole punch to punch 8 evenly spaced holes on plain long sides for lacing together. To match holes, punch one cover first, put punched one on top, and use pencil to mark holes on bottom piece. Punch holes at pencil marks.

For grass on bottom of journal, cut ¾"x6" kelly green strip. Trim top with rotary cutter and wave blade so piece is ½"x6". Glue on bottom of cover.

4 For basket, measure sides and adjust patterns if needed. Glue on outside and inside of basket.

5 For flower stems, cut ⅛" kelly green strips with rotary cutter and wavy blade. Cut different lengths with scissors as needed.

Attach a clothespin to hold notes!

A basket will hold lots of stuff!

A can is the perfect pen and pencil holder!

ASSEMBLE

1 See photo. Glue stems on projects. Add flowers on top of stems, and glue centers on flowers. Glue leaves next to stems. Glue buttons randomly around flowers. On note holder, glue mini clothespin next to rim of can. Glue blue tinsel pom pom on clothespin.

2 Use Soft Blue paint pen to write "My Journal" on cover of journal. Use both colors of paint pen to write words on 2 basket ends. Some suggestions are: Pencils, Paper Clips, Rubber Stamps, Stuff, Notes, or Do Not Touch.

3 Glue narrow ribbon around tops of both cans and on top and corners of basket.

4 Use paper cutter to cut paper in half. Punch holes in paper to match covers. Thread pink ribbon through tapestry needle and lace book together. Tie bow at top. For a bookmark, glue pink tinsel pom pom on one end of 12" of piece pink ribbon. Tie other end next to bow at top of journal. ◼

Patterns on page 66.

Project on page 64.

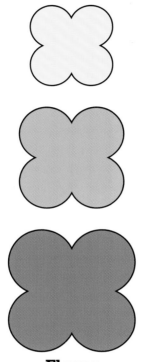

Flower
Cut as many as
needed from assorted colors
of thin craft foam

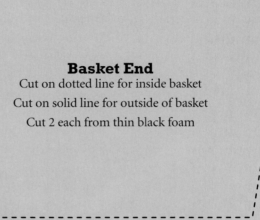

Basket End
Cut on dotted line for inside basket

Cut on solid line for outside of basket

Cut 2 each from thin black foam

Leaves
Cut as many as
needed from kelly green
thin craft foam

Flower Centers
Cut as many as
needed from assorted colors
of thin craft foam

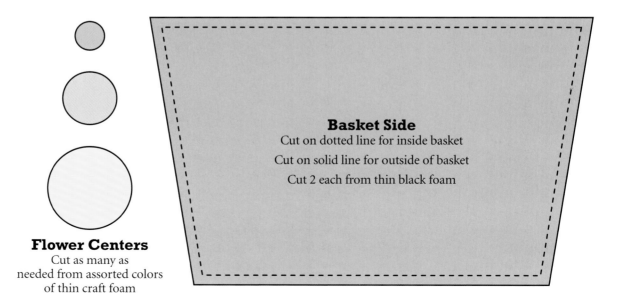

Basket Side
Cut on dotted line for inside basket

Cut on solid line for outside of basket

Cut 2 each from thin black foam

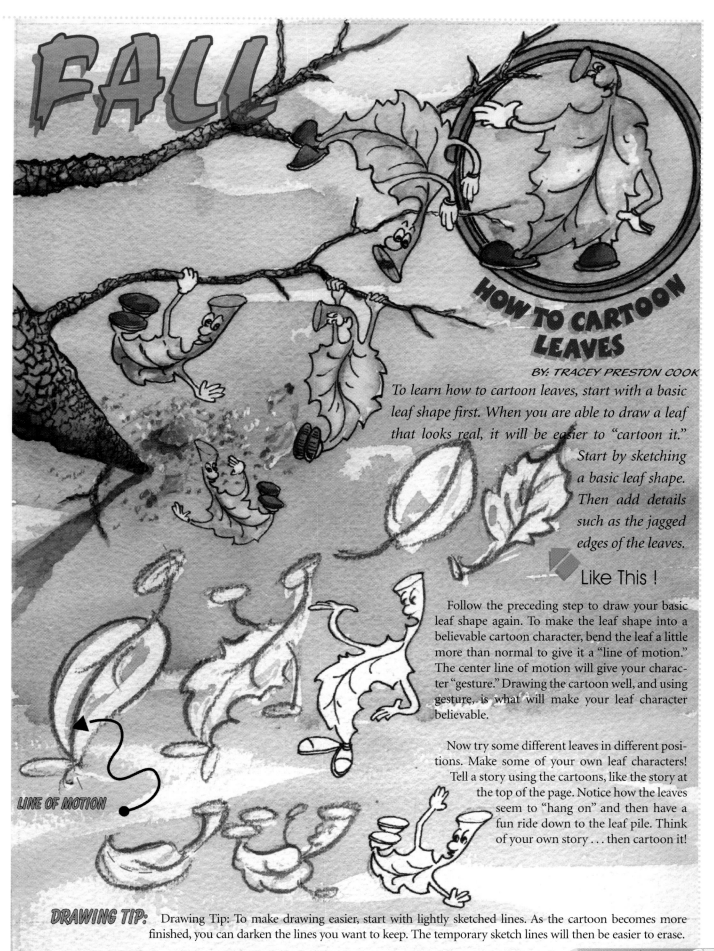

FALL

HOW TO CARTOON LEAVES

BY: TRACEY PRESTON COOK

To learn how to cartoon leaves, start with a basic leaf shape first. When you are able to draw a leaf that looks real, it will be easier to "cartoon it."

Start by sketching a basic leaf shape. Then add details such as the jagged edges of the leaves.

Like This!

Follow the preceding step to draw your basic leaf shape again. To make the leaf shape into a believable cartoon character, bend the leaf a little more than normal to give it a "line of motion." The center line of motion will give your character "gesture." Drawing the cartoon well, and using gesture, is what will make your leaf character believable.

Now try some different leaves in different positions. Make some of your own leaf characters! Tell a story using the cartoons, like the story at the top of the page. Notice how the leaves seem to "hang on" and then have a fun ride down to the leaf pile. Think of your own story . . . then cartoon it!

LINE OF MOTION

DRAWING TIP: Drawing Tip: To make drawing easier, start with lightly sketched lines. As the cartoon becomes more finished, you can darken the lines you want to keep. The temporary sketch lines will then be easier to erase.

THANKSGIVING CANDY CORN WREATH

by Annabelle Keller

MATERIALS

- 12" diameter plastic-foam wreath*
- Ten 2"x3" plastic-foam cones
- Three 2"x4" plastic-foam cones
- Acrylic paint*: Opaque Yellow, Magnolia White, Pumpkin, Spice Brown
- 12"x24" poster board
- 1 package brown paper ribbon
- 1 package each ⅜" raffia ribbon: orange, brown
- 18" length of floral wire
- Candle stub or paraffin
- Glue gun, serrated knife, paintbrush, pencil, scissors, wax paper, yardstick

* The following products were used for this project: Styrofoam® plastic foam · Delta Ceramcoat® Acrylic Paints · MPR#9 PapeRibbon-Kraft.

INSTRUCTIONS

☺ Adult supervision is needed when using glue gun and knife.

1 Trace inner and outer edges of wreath twice on poster board. Cut out circles. Glue one circle on each side of wreath. Glue end of paper ribbon on back of wreath. Wrap paper around wreath, gluing in place every 3 inches. Cover entire wreath.

For hanger, fold wire in half, forming a 1" loop. Twist together below loop. Wrap wire around wreath over paper ribbon ends.

2 For bow, cut five orange and five brown 1½ yard lengths of raffia. Hold strands together and make a 4-loop bow with 4" loops and 11" tails. Twist wire around center of strands. Curl tails by scraping strands with edge of scissors. Twist wire around top center of wreath.

3 For candy corn, cut foam cones in half vertically. Run knife back and forth through wax as needed to make cutting easier. Sand any rough edges by rubbing halves together.

See photo. Paint cones with white, orange, brown, and yellow stripes to resemble candy corn. Set on wax paper to dry. Paint brown faces on two large cones and a yellow face on one small cone. Let dry.

4 Glue two large cones with faces at the 3:00 and 8:00 positions and one small cone at 6:00 position. Arrange and glue remaining cones on wreath. ■

SWEET WREATHS

by Christine Bando

MATERIALS
- ▶ Round sugar cookies (purchased or homemade)
- ▶ Frosting:
  2 cups powdered sugar
  ½ tablespoon butter
  ⅛ teaspoon vanilla
  2 drops food coloring
  milk (as needed)
- ▶ Candy corn
- ▶ Red licorice whips
- ▶ Butter knife, mixing bowl, spoon

INSTRUCTIONS

1 To make frosting, pour powdered sugar into mixing bowl. Melt butter and mix with sugar. Add vanilla and 1 to 2 drops food coloring. Mix together. Add milk 1 teaspoon at a time until frosting is spreadable.

2 Using butter knife, spread frosting in a ring around cookie, leaving center unfrosted. Scatter candy corn around cookie, pushing candy into frosting.

3 Tie 8" strip of licorice into a bow. *Note: If licorice is too sticky, wet fingertips with water to dampen licorice strips.* Dab a little frosting on back of bow and stick on cookie. Refrigerate to harden frosting. ■

CANDY APPLES

MATERIALS
- ▶ 6 to 8 apples
- ▶ 1¼ cups of sugar
- ▶ 1 cup light corn syrup
- ▶ 1 craft stick for each apple
- ▶ Cooking pot, measuring cup, wax paper, wooden mixing spoon

INSTRUCTIONS

☺ Adult supervision is needed when cooking.

1 Push a craft stick into the stem of each apple. Spread wax paper on counter. Mix sugar with corn syrup. Cook over a medium heat. Stir when mixture begins to boil. The mixture will take 20 to 30 minutes to cook, but must be checked often after 15 minutes. With spoon, drop a small amount of mixture into a cup of cold water. If mixture is done, the candy ball that forms should be hard and brittle. Continue to check every 5 minutes.

2 When the candy mixture is done, coat apples. Hold each apple by its stick and dip and turn apple in mixture until it is coated with candy. Place the coated apple on the wax paper with the stick up. Let it cool and harden. ■

SCARECROW DOOR HANGER

by Debi Goldfisher

MATERIALS
- ▸ 3"x9½" wood door hanger
- ▸ Felt*: 6"x8" cashmere tan, 3"x5" gold, 4"x6" light blue, scraps of black and yellow
- ▸ Acorn Brown acrylic paint*
- ▸ Acrylic spray sealer
- ▸ #8 flat paintbrush
- ▸ Embroidery floss: dark blue, black
- ▸ 4 fall pattern ribbon scraps
- ▸ 2½" of ⅛" red cord
- ▸ Two ¼" black pom poms
- ▸ Polyester fiberfill
- ▸ Wood excelsior
- ▸ Buttons: two ⅜", one ½"
- ▸ Two 5mm wiggle eyes
- ▸ Two black seed beads
- ▸ 3" straw hat
- ▸ Black fine-line permanent marker
- ▸ Thick craft glue
- ▸ Brown paper bag, needle, paper plate, pencil, pinking shears, sandpaper, scissors, straight pins, toothpick, tracing paper, water container

* The following products were used for this project: Kunin Classic Rainbow™ Felt · Plaid FolkArt® acrylic paint.

Figure 1

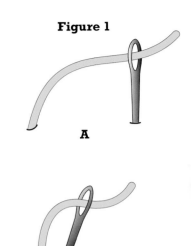

A

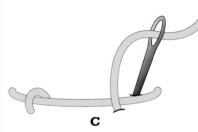

B

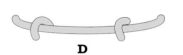

C

D

INSTRUCTIONS

- ☺ Trace and cut out patterns. Follow directions.
- ☺ Use 2 strands of floss for all stitching.

1 Sand door hanger. Paint front and edges with two coats Acorn Brown. Use marker to draw stitch lines around edges of doorknob opening and outside edges of hanger. Spray with a coat of acrylic sealer. Rub surface with a piece of paper bag to smooth.

2 Pin shirt on body. Use blue floss to sew running stitch around edge of shirt. Pin overalls on body. Use blue floss to sew running stitch around edge of overalls, leaving an opening for stuffing. Stuff lightly with fiberfill. Stitch opening closed.

3 Cut four ½" ribbon squares with pinking shears. Glue patches on front of overalls. Glue ⅜" button on each overall strap.

4 Use black floss to backstitch mouth. See Figure 1. Sew three small straight stitches along mouth to shape smile. For eyes, glue seed beads on face, using toothpick to apply glue. Cut ¼" fringe in ends of arms and legs.

5 Glue scarecrow on door hanger below hole. For hair, glue several strands of excelsior on top of head. Trim to desired length. Cut straw hat in half and glue over hair. Glue a button on each top corner of hanger.

6 Glue red cord along brim of hat. Trim excess. For crow's tail, cut a tiny black triangle. Glue on bottom of black body pom pom. For crow's beak, cut a tiny yellow triangle. Glue on top of body pom pom. Glue head pom pom on top of triangle. Glue wiggle eyes above beak. ■

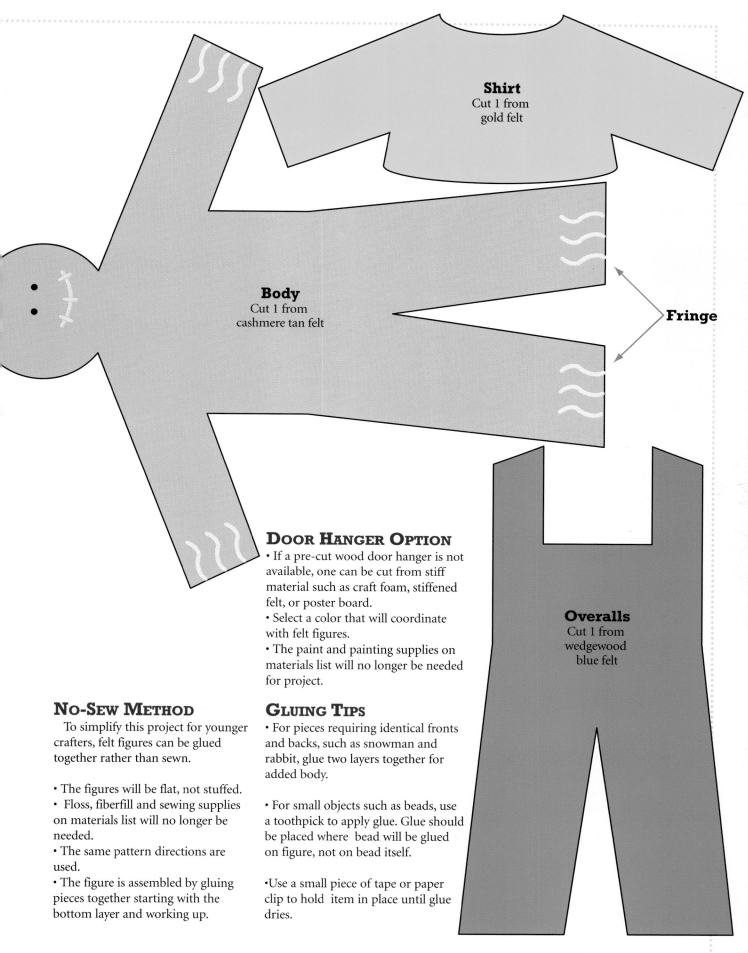

Shirt
Cut 1 from gold felt

Body
Cut 1 from cashmere tan felt

Fringe

Overalls
Cut 1 from wedgewood blue felt

DOOR HANGER OPTION

• If a pre-cut wood door hanger is not available, one can be cut from stiff material such as craft foam, stiffened felt, or poster board.
• Select a color that will coordinate with felt figures.
• The paint and painting supplies on materials list will no longer be needed for project.

NO-SEW METHOD

To simplify this project for younger crafters, felt figures can be glued together rather than sewn.

• The figures will be flat, not stuffed.
• Floss, fiberfill and sewing supplies on materials list will no longer be needed.
• The same pattern directions are used.
• The figure is assembled by gluing pieces together starting with the bottom layer and working up.

GLUING TIPS

• For pieces requiring identical fronts and backs, such as snowman and rabbit, glue two layers together for added body.

• For small objects such as beads, use a toothpick to apply glue. Glue should be placed where bead will be glued on figure, not on bead itself.

• Use a small piece of tape or paper clip to hold item in place until glue dries.

"ALL WRAPPED UP" MUMMY

*by Cindy Groom Harry®
and Staff*

MATERIALS

- ►Adjustable air freshener*
- ►2" plastic foam ball*
- ►12"x36" muslin (or old white sheet)
- ►1½"x4" piece ivory felt*
- ►Red dimensional paint*
- ►Ivory acrylic paint*
- ►#6 flat paintbrush*
- ►1"x1½" oval wood craft shape*
- ►Straight pin with large head
- ►Two 12mm wiggle eyes
- ►Two 12" white jumbo chenille stems
- ►½"-wide double stick tape
- ►1"x1½" mini pumpkin
- ►Two black plastic spiders
- ►Serrated knife
- ►Thick craft glue
- ►Plastic wrap, pencil, ruler, scissors, wire cutter

* The following products were used for this project: Dial Renuzit® Long Last™ Adjustable Air Freshener* · Styrofoam® Brand plastic foam ball · Kunin Felt/Foss Rainbow™ Felt · Duncan Scribbles® 3-Dimensional Fabric Writer · Aleene's® Premium Coat™ acrylic paint · Forster® Woodsies™ oval · Loew-Cornell® paintbrush.

INSTRUCTIONS

☺ Adult supervision is needed when working with serrated knife.

☺ Trace and cut out pattern. Follow directions.

1 For head, use serrated knife to cut a slice off bottom of foam ball. For face, cut a 1½" felt square with rounded corners. With cut side of ball down, glue felt on front of foam ball. Glue wiggle eyes on face. For nose, dip head of pin in ivory paint. When

Mouth Painting Guide

Hand
Cut 2 from
ivory felt

dry, push nose pin into face. For mouth, tape plastic wrap over mouth pattern. Trace pattern on plastic wrap using red dimensional paint. When dry, peel mouth from plastic and glue on face.

2 To wrap head, tear four ½"x36" fabric strips. Use double-stick tape to hold end of fabric on head. Begin wrapping a length of fabric around head. Cross wraps over one another, covering edges of felt, and one eye. Continue wrapping strips, covering entire head. Glue end of strip. Set wrapped head aside.

3 For body, stick tape on air freshener top and base as follows: one 5" strip around top; one 10" strip around bottom; three 3" vertical strips evenly spaced around top; two 10" strips, one around top and other around bottom of base. To wrap top, tear four ½"x36" fabric strips. Wrap strips around top same as for head. Glue head on body. To wrap base, tear two ½"x36" fabric strips. Wrap base same as for top.

4 For feet, use scissors to cut wood oval in half. Stick a 1" piece of tape on each side of each piece. Tear a ½"x36" fabric strip. Cut into two 18" strips. Wrap one strip around each

foot until completely covered, taping ends of strips. Glue feet on bottom front of base, moving fabric so wood is glued on base.

5 For arms, use wire cutter to cut two 9" pieces chenille stem. Loosely twist stems together. Glue one hand on each end of arms with thumbs pointing up. To wrap arms, tear six ½"x36" fabric strips. Loosely wrap strips around chenille stems, having strips cross over one another and using tape to hold ends in place. Find center of arms and glue on back of body at neck. Bend arms to front.

6 Glue pumpkin on tummy. Glue hands on pumpkin. Glue one spider on head and one on foot. ■

TO REFRESHEN GEL
Replace original air-freshener gel when it is depleted with a new container base. If project base is decorated, remove dried gel. From new container, remove new, non-toxic gel. Slip it over post of base and reposition decorated topper.

For FREE Renuzit® Adjustable Air Freshener Craft Project Sheets, send $1 for postage and handling and a long self-addressed envelope to: Renuzit® Crafts, Cindy Groom-Harry®, 2363 - 460th St., Dept. GAM-Mummy, Ireton, IA 51027.

Halloween Masks

by Paula Bales

Materials For All
- ► Fuchsia acrylic paint*
- ► #4 bristle paintbrush
- ► Medium-point black marker*
- ► ¼"-wide elastic
- ► Craft knife
- ► Hot glue gun and glue sticks
- ► Thick craft glue
- ► Paper towels, pencil, scissors, tracing paper

For Giraffe
- ► Craft foam: yellow, orange, brown, pink
- ► Two ½" black buttons

For Chimp
- ► Craft foam: brown, light brown, pink
- ► Thick craft foam: black

For Zebra
- ► White and black craft foam
- ► Two ½" buttons
- ► 48" hot pink embroidery floss

For Lion
- ► Orange and tan craft foam
- ► Thick black craft foam

* The following products were used for this project: DecoArt™ acrylic paint · ZIG® Memory System .08 Millennium Pen · Loew Cornell paintbrush.

Instructions
- ☺ Adult supervision needed when working with craft knife and hot glue gun.
- ☺ Trace and cut out patterns. Follow directions.
- ☺ Use scissors to cut out masks, craft knife to cut out eye holes.

1 For Giraffe, paint cheeks by dabbing bristle brush in paint. Dab paint off on paper towel, then on cheeks. Use marker to outline all pieces.

To assemble, use craft glue to glue pieces on head as follows: spots, inner ears, and mane. Glue horns on back of head. For nostrils, glue buttons on head. Measure elastic to fit around head and hot glue each end to sides of mask. See photo. Use marker to add face details.

2 For Chimp, paint cheeks and outline pieces same as for Giraffe. To assemble, use craft glue to glue pieces on head as follows: face, nose, inner ears. Add elastic same as for Giraffe. See photo. Use marker to add face details.

3 For Zebra, paint cheeks and outline pieces same as for Giraffe. To assemble, use craft glue to glue pieces as follows: stripes, topknot. For nostrils, glue buttons on head. Add elastic same as for Giraffe. See photo. Use marker to add face details. Cut floss into four 12" lengths. Hold lengths together and tie in bow. Glue bow on top center of head.

4 For Lion, paint cheeks and outline same as for Giraffe. To assemble, use craft glue to glue pieces as follows: face, nose, eyebrows. See photo. Use marker to add face details. ■

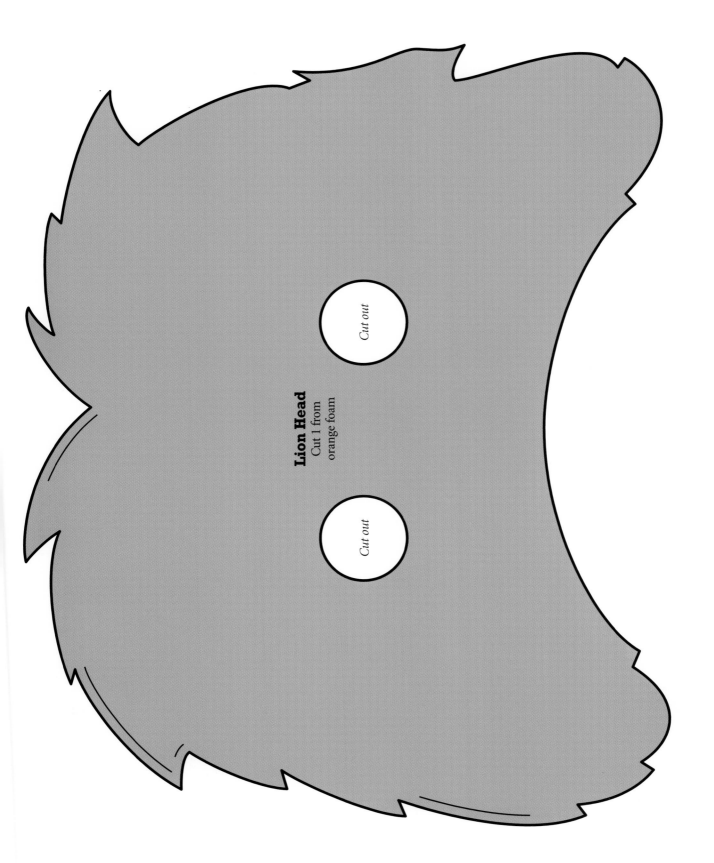

Lion Head
Cut 1 from
orange foam

Cut out

Cut out

Additional patterns for Lion are on page 77

Giraffe found on page 78.

Chimp Head
Cut 1 from
brown foam

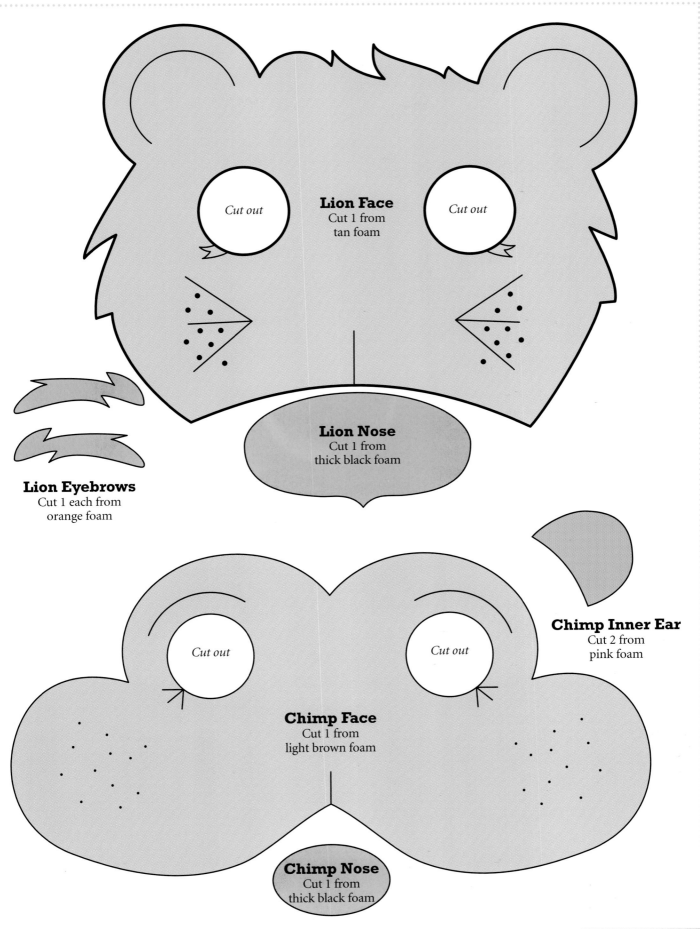

Lion Face
Cut 1 from
tan foam

Cut out

Cut out

Lion Eyebrows
Cut 1 each from
orange foam

Lion Nose
Cut 1 from
thick black foam

Chimp Inner Ear
Cut 2 from
pink foam

Chimp Face
Cut 1 from
light brown foam

Cut out

Cut out

Chimp Nose
Cut 1 from
thick black foam

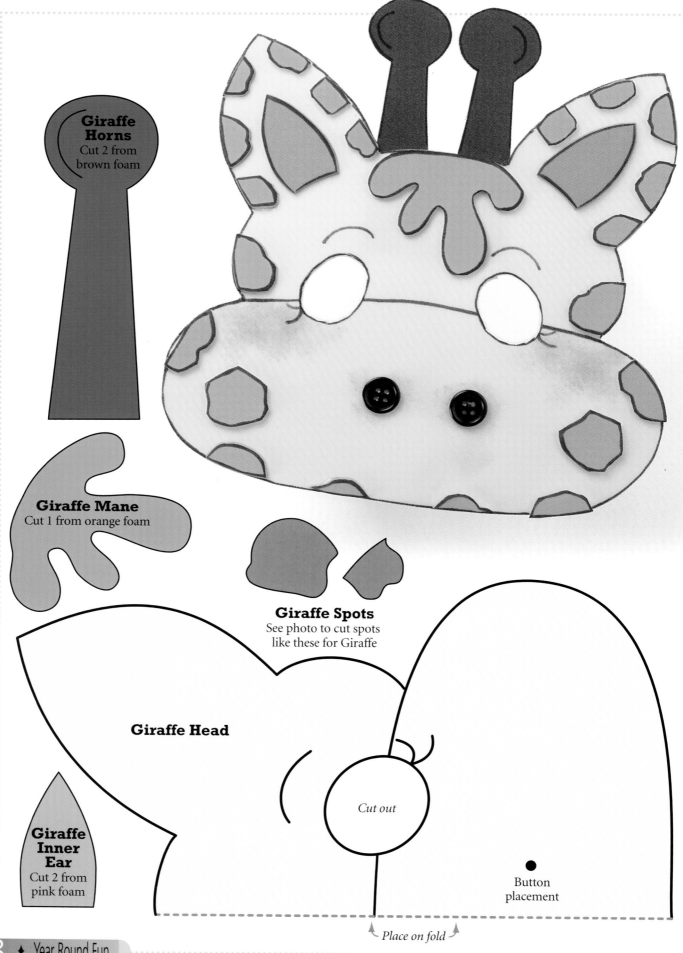

Giraffe Horns
Cut 2 from
brown foam

Giraffe Mane
Cut 1 from orange foam

Giraffe Spots
See photo to cut spots
like these for Giraffe

Giraffe Head

Giraffe Inner Ear
Cut 2 from
pink foam

Cut out

●
Button
placement

⌃ *Place on fold* ⌃

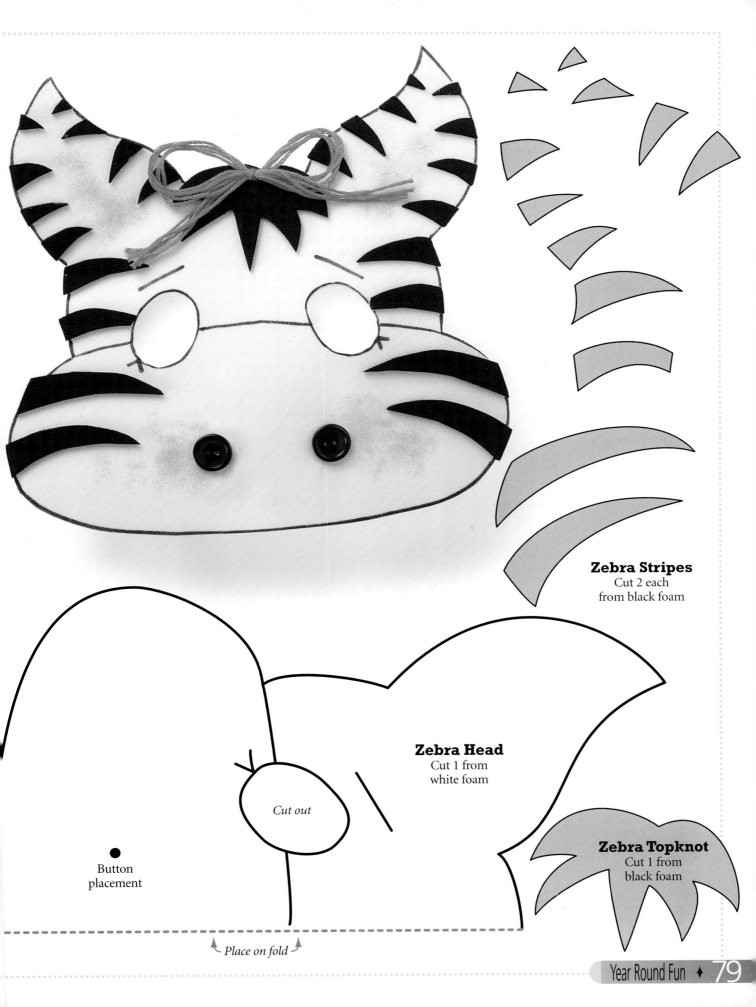

Zebra Stripes
Cut 2 each
from black foam

Zebra Head
Cut 1 from
white foam

Cut out

●
Button
placement

Zebra Topknot
Cut 1 from
black foam

Place on fold

Halloween Party Favors

by Mary T. Cosgrove

Make a pencil topper!

Instead of attaching the 4" chenille stem on the bag, wind it around the top of a pencil.

Materials

- 8¾"x12" lime green felt
- 6 yards of orange ribbon floss*
  Optional: embroidery floss
- Chenille stems: 2 white, 3 orange, 3 black
- Embroidery needle
- Two 10mm wiggle eyes
- Wire cutter
- Thick craft glue
- Pencils (optional)
- *Optional: 1" of ½" magnetic strip*
- **Candy or treats**
- Pencil, tracing paper

* *Rhode Island Textile Co. RibbonFloss™ was used for this project.*

Instructions

☺ Trace patterns. Follow directions.

Bags

1 For treat bags, cut felt into three 4"x8¾" pieces. Fold each in half with short edges at top.

2 Cut 1 yard ribbon floss. Thread on embroidery needle and knot ends together. Starting at top of bag, whipstitch one side and knot at inside of bottom. Repeat on other side. Leave top edge open.

For drawstring, cut 1 yard ribbon floss. Beginning and ending at center front of pouch, gather stitch all the way around bag. Remove needle. Pull ends evenly. Follow instructions on next page to make chenille stem shapes. Wind stem of character around center back stitch of bag. Fill bag with candy or treats. Pull floss to gather pouch and tie in a bow.

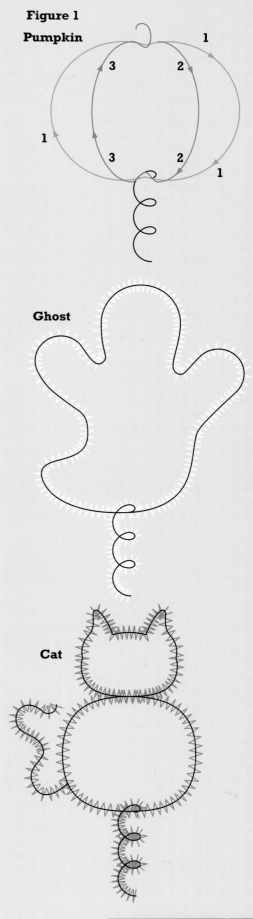

Figure 1
Pumpkin

Ghost

Cat

Make a photo magnet!

Glue a child's photo on the back of the chenille head. Tie a floss ribbon around the neck and add a small magnet strip on the back of the head.

STEM SHAPES

1 Ghost. Bend chenille stem in half to find the center. See Figure 1. Begin shaping ghost by matching center of stem with top center of head. Shape ghost using pattern as guide. At bottom, cut off extra and twist ends around each other. Cut a 4" length of white stem. Wind one end around bottom of ghost.

2 Pumpkin. See Figure 1. Shape pumpkin using pattern as guide, making outside circle and wrapping beginning end around stem at top center. To form inside curves, wind stem over front, behind and under bottom of pumpkin. Wind once at bottom. Bring stem back up to top. Wind over center top of pumpkin and trim to form a ½" pumpkin stem. Cut a 4" length of orange stem. Wind one end around bottom of pumpkin.

To add a face on pumpkin, glue outside edge of each of wiggle eye on inside curves ¾" down from top. For smile, glue ends of a 12" piece of orange ribbon floss or embroidery floss on back of wiggle eyes.

3 Cat. Bend chenille stem in half to find the center. See Figure 1. Begin shaping cat by matching center of stem with top center of head. Shape cat using pattern as guide. Twist stems together at bottom of head, then shape body. Bring ends over to one side and twist together. Cut one 2" long for tail and other close to body. Shape tail. Cut a 4" length of black stem. Wind one end around bottom of cat. ■

VAMPIRE CANDY CAN

by Helen Rafson

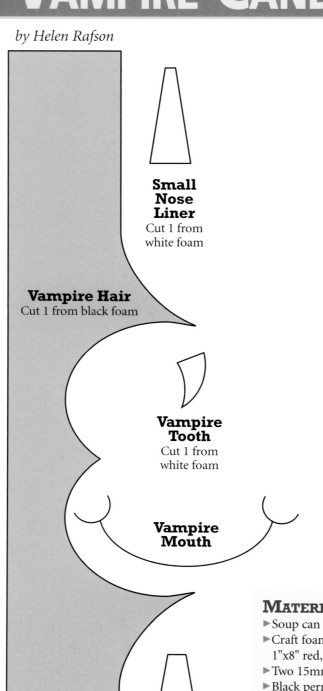

Small Nose Liner
Cut 1 from white foam

Vampire Hair
Cut 1 from black foam

Vampire Tooth
Cut 1 from white foam

Vampire Mouth

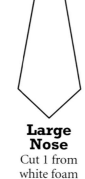

Large Nose
Cut 1 from white foam

MATERIALS

- Soup can
- Craft foam: 2"x9" black, 1"x8" red, 4"x10"white
- Two 15mm wiggle eyes
- Black permanent markers: fine-tip, medium-tip
- Craft foam glue*
- Pencil, ruler, scissors, tracing paper

* Craft Foam Glue from the Beacon Chemical Company was used for this project.

INSTRUCTIONS

☺ Trace and cut out patterns. Follow directions.

1 Remove label from soup can. Clean and dry can.

2 Cut 4"x8½" piece of white foam for head. Glue foam around can. Cut 1"x7¾" piece of red foam for cape. Cut ends at an angle. Glue around bottom of can.

3 Glue hair, eyes, and eyebrows on head. Glue large nose over small nose liner to make it pop out. Glue nose on face.

4 Draw mouth with black medium-point marker. Outline teeth with a fine-tip marker. Glue on teeth. ■

by Helen Rafson

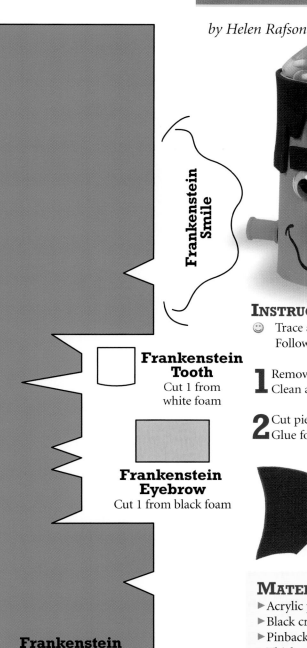

Frankenstein Smile

Frankenstein Tooth
Cut 1 from white foam

Frankenstein Eyebrow
Cut 1 from black foam

Frankenstein Hair
Cut 1 from green foam

MATERIALS
- ▶ Soup can
- ▶ Craft foam: green, black, white
- ▶ Two 15mm wiggle eyes
- ▶ Two ⅝" wooden spools
- ▶ Green acrylic paint
- ▶ Black permanent marker
- ▶ ¾" green pom pom
- ▶ Craft foam glue*
- ▶ Paintbrush, pencil, ruler, scissors, tracing paper

* Craft Foam Glue from the Beacon Chemical Company was used for this project.

INSTRUCTIONS
☺ Trace and cut out patterns. Follow directions.

1 Remove label from soup can. Clean and dry can.

2 Cut piece of green foam 4"x8½". Glue foam board around can.

3 Glue on hair, eyes, and eyebrows.

4 Use black marker to draw mouth. Glue on tooth. Glue on nose.

5 Paint wooden spools green. Let dry. Glue a spool on each side of head. ◼

BAT PIN

by Paula Bales

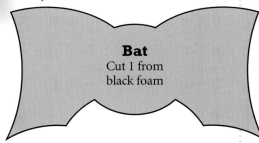

Bat
Cut 1 from black foam

MATERIALS
- ▶ Acrylic paint: white, red, black
- ▶ Black craft foam
- ▶ Pinback
- ▶ Thick craft glue
- ▶ Paper towels, pencil, small paintbrush, scissors, straight pin, toothpicks, tracing paper

INSTRUCTIONS
☺ Trace and cut out pattern. Follow directions.

1 Use end of paintbrush to dot eyes white. Use a toothpick to dot pupils black and nose red.

2 To paint cheeks red, dab paint off onto paper towel and then onto cheeks and ear centers. Paint mouth white.

3 Glue pinback on back of pin. ◼

BOO BUDDIES T-SHIRT

by Paula Bales

MATERIALS
▸ Child's orange T-shirt
▸ Fabric paint*: black, white, orange
▸ White acrylic paint
▸ #4 bristle paintbrush
▸ Painting sponges*
▸ Large household sponge
▸ T-shirt board or cardboard from cereal box
▸ Medium-point black marker*
▸ Cotton swabs, paper plate, paper towels, pencil, scissors, toothpick, tracing paper

* The following products were used for this project: Tulip Slick fabric paint · DecoArt™ Americana acrylic paint · ZIG® Memory System™ 08 Millennium marker.

INSTRUCTIONS
☺ Trace and cut out patterns. Follow directions.
☺ See photo for design placement.

1 To cut sponge shapes, dampen sponge. Wring out extra water. Use marker to trace patterns on sponge. Cut out. Rinse marker out of sponge and squeeze to remove water.

2 Slide T-shirt board inside shirt. Squeeze white paint on paper plate. Dab sponge in paint and then on T-shirt. Repeat for other face. Let dry.

3 For ghost faces, squeeze black and orange paint on paper plate. Dab eye/mouth sponge in black and press on eyes and one mouth. Dip nose sponge in orange and press on noses. For ghost cheeks, dab bristle brush in orange paint. Dab off paint onto paper towel and then on cheeks.

4 For spiders, dip spider sponge in black and press spiders on shirt. For eyes, dip eraser end of pencil in white and dot two spider eyes. Dip end of toothpick in black to add dots on spider eyes. Dip cotton swab in orange and dab spider noses.

5 Use black fabric paint to add spider legs, web lines, smile on face, and lettering. Make black dots on ends of legs and letters with cotton swab. Follow manufacturer's directions for heat-setting fabric paint on shirt. ∎

Boo! Buddies

Face
Cut 1 from sponge

Spider
Cut 1 from sponge

Eye/ Mouth
Cut 1 from sponge

Nose
Cut 1 from sponge

Smile

PAPER-STRIP PUMPKIN

by Mary Strouse

These 3-dimensional pumpkins are wobbly fun. They can't be pushed over. If you keep them, you'll never be broke . . . because a penny is used for weight!

MATERIALS FOR ONE

- ▶ Three 1"x12" strips of orange construction paper
- ▶ One 1"x1½" strip green construction paper
- ▶ ½ sheet black construction paper
- ▶ Penny
- ▶ Thick craft glue
- ▶ Pencil, scissors, tracing paper

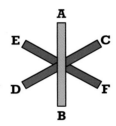

Figure 1

INSTRUCTIONS

☺ Trace and cut out patterns. Follow directions.

1 See Figure 1. Glue orange strips together in centers. Glue AB over CD, then over EF. Have equal distance between strips.

Overlap and glue E & F ends together forming a circle. Repeat for A & B, then C & D.

2 Roll green strip into a stem. Cut small slits in bottom of stem⅛" apart. Glue cut end of stem on top of pumpkin. For weight, glue penny on center bottom of pumpkin.

3 Glue eyes, nose, and mouth on pumpkin. ■

Pumpkin Face
Cut 1 of each piece
from black
construction paper

CLAY POT TURKEY

by Helen Rafson

MATERIALS

- 2¼" clay pot
- Brown craft foam
- Wood craft shapes*: ⅛"x¾" heart*, two 1¼" stars*
- Acrylic paint: brown, tan, rust, orange
- Matte acrylic spray sealer
- 1¾" red chenille stem
- 3 red silk leaves
- Two 12mm wiggle eyes
- 6" twine
- Lint-free cloth
- Black permanent fine-tip marker
- Thick craft glue
- Paintbrush, paper plate, pencil, pinking shears, ruler, sandpaper, scissors, sponge, tracing paper

* The following products were used for this project: Lara's Crafts wood hearts · Forster® Woodsies™ wood stars.

INSTRUCTIONS

☺ Trace and cut out patterns. Follow directions.

☺ Let paint dry completely after each coat.

1 Sand rough edges of clay pot. Remove dust with cloth. Paint inside and outside of pot with 2 coats of brown paint.

2 Pour puddles of tan and rust paint on paper plate. Dip sponge in water. Wring out as much water as possible. Dip sponge in both colors and sponge on outside of pot. Use paintbrush to paint stars and heart with 2 coats of orange paint.

3 Spray sealer on inside and outside of pot, heart, and stars.

4 With fine-tip marker, draw "stitch" lines around stars, heart, and wings. See photo. Glue on eyes, beak, feet, and wings. For wattle, fold chenille stem into a cane and glue above beak. For tail, remove stems from leaves. Glue 3 leaves together in a fan shape. Glue leaves on back of pot.

5 Tie twine in a bow. Glue on bottom front of turkey. ■

Turkey Wing
Cut 2 from brown foam with pinking shears

Turkey Magnet

by Paula Bales

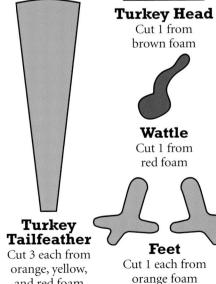

Head Feathers
Cut 1 from orange foam

Beak
Cut 1 from yellow foam

Turkey Head
Cut 1 from brown foam

Wattle
Cut 1 from red foam

Turkey Tailfeather
Cut 3 each from orange, yellow, and red foam

Feet
Cut 1 each from orange foam

MATERIALS

- ▶ 2⅛" metal end from biscuit can
- ▶ Spray metal primer
- ▶ Acrylic paint: brown, red, black
- ▶ Craft foam: brown, orange, yellow, red
- ▶ Fine-line permanent marker
- ▶ Self-adhering magnet strip
- ▶ Thick craft glue
- ▶ Paintbrush, pencil, scissors, tracing paper

INSTRUCTIONS

☺ Trace and cut out patterns. Follow directions.
☺ Let paint dry between coats.

1 Spray can end with metal primer. Let dry. Dab on brown paint.

Paint turkey head brown. See photo. With marker, draw lines around head, beak, wattle, head feathers, body, and feet. Add dots on beaks and lines on feet.

2 Glue beak over wattle. Glue wattle on head. Glue head feathers on head. Use end of paintbrush handle to dot eyes with black. Draw eyebrows with marker.

3 Glue head on front of body. Glue feet and 9 feathers on back of body. With marker, draw curved lines and 4 dots on each tail feather. Glue magnet strip on back of turkey.

Option: *Glue pinback on back of turkey and wear as pin.* ◼

PILGRIM CLOTHESPIN DOLLS

by Nancy Bell Anderson

MATERIALS FOR ALL
- ▶ Wood craft pieces*: doll pin, 2 craft picks
- ▶ Acrylic paint*: black, red, white
- ▶ Small paintbrush
- ▶ Thick craft glue
- ▶ Pencil, scissors, tracing paper

FOR PILGRIM LADY
- ▶ Pink acrylic paint*
- ▶ Broadcloth fabric: 5"x6" white, 4"x8" gray
- ▶ 8" of ⅛" white satin ribbon
- ▶ Dark brown curly doll hair*
- ▶ Needle, thread
- ▶ *Optional: fray check liquid**

FOR PILGRIM MAN
- ▶ Silver acrylic paint*
- ▶ Fabric: 3"x5" gray broadcloth, 4"x6" brown suede*, 2"x4" black felt
- ▶ 2½" of ¼" black ribbon
- ▶ Dark brown curly doll hair*
- ▶ Fray check liquid (optional)*
- ▶ Small piece white paper

FOR INDIAN
- ▶ Craft pick*
- ▶ Burnt Umber acrylic paint*
- ▶ 3"x4" tan suede*, scraps contrasting color of suede
- ▶ 1 yard black yarn
- ▶ 5 - 6 small feathers

* The following products were used for this project: Forster® wood craft pieces · DecoArt™ Americana™ acrylic paint · C.W. Fifield Co., Inc. and Tandy suede · All Cooped Up doll hair · Dritz® Fray Check™.

INSTRUCTIONS
☺ Trace and cut out patterns. Follow directions.

PILGRIM LADY
1 See Figure 1. Use small paintbrush to paint red mouth, pink cheeks, and black nose, eyes, and eyebrows. Add tiny white highlights on eyes. For shoes, paint bottom ½" of doll pin black.

Figure 1

2 *Optional: Put fray check liquid on all cut edges of fabric.* Glue pantaloons around doll, tucking between front and back of legs.

3 For dress, gather stitch each end of sleeve. Pull up gathers so sleeves measure ⅞". Knot and clip thread. With right sides together, sew underarm and side seams with running stitch. Slash at underarm and center back where shown on pattern. Turn to right side. Put dress on doll. Glue at neckline. Glue back opening closed. Tie a piece of thread tightly around waist.

4 For apron, drape straps over shoulders, crossing them at front and back. Glue on shoulder and at front and back waist. Gather stitch apron top and pull gathers so apron measures ¾". Knot and clip thread. Center and glue white ribbon on apron top, covering

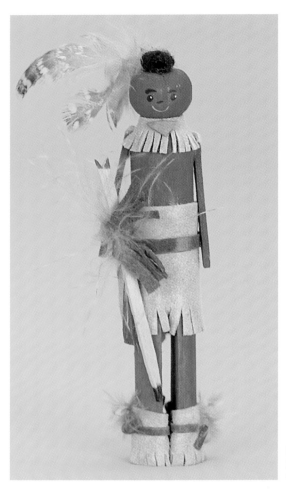

Dress an Indian brave in suede leather and feathers.

gather stitches. Tie apron around waist with a bow at center back. Put a drop of glue on center of bow. Trim ribbon ends at a slant.

For arms, cut 1⅛" off round end of craft picks. Discard long piece. Put glue on cut end of craft picks and insert into sleeves.

5 Glue small amount of doll hair on head. For hat, cut on slash lines as shown on pattern. Fold outside ends to middle and glue. Glue hat on head.

PILGRIM MAN

1 Use small paintbrush to paint face. Paint black dot eyes. For eyebrows, paint short black line above eyes. For nose, paint short black line. Add tiny white highlights on eyes. Paint a "v" shaped red mouth. For shoes, paint bottom ½" of doll pin black. Paint silver buckles on boots. Paint 2 other buckles silver.

2 For knickers, gather stitch at cuffs and pull up gathers so cuffs measure 1⅛". Knot and clip thread. Glue around doll's legs. Glue cuff bands over gathers on each leg.

3 For jacket, cut fringe on sleeve and jacket hems. Put jacket over doll's head. Glue front over back at sides and underarms. Overlap and glue along center front. Tie a piece of thread tightly around waist. For belt, glue black ribbon around waist. Glue buckle on front of belt. Glue collar around neck.

For arms, cut 1⅛" off round end of craft picks. Discard long piece. Put glue on end of craft picks and insert into sleeves.

4 Glue hair on head and tiny mustache and beard on face. For hat, glue short ends of hat together

forming a tube. Glue tube on center of brim. Glue top on center of hat. Glue hat on doll's head. Glue buckle on center front of hat.

INDIAN

1 For arms, cut 1⅛" off round end of craft picks. Save one long piece for spear. Paint arms and body. When dry, paint face same as for Pilgrim man.

2 For loincloth, cut a 1½"x2½" brown suede rectangle. Cut ⅛" fringe along one long side. Cut some ⅛" leather strips from contrasting suede. Wrap and glue loincloth around waist. Tie on one side with contrasting strip of leather.

Glue arms on shoulders. For collar, cut ⅜"x1¾" brown suede rectangle. Fringe one long side. Glue collar around neck. Glue contrasting suede triangle on collar. For leggings, cut two ½"x1½" brown suede rectangles. Fringe one long side on each one. Glue legging around each lower leg. Tie small contrasting leather strip around each legging. Glue tiny feathers at knots.

3 Tie ends of three 12" pieces of black yarn together and braid for 2½". Glue tiny leather strip around end of braid. Trim close to knot at beginning of braid and glue knot on head. Glue feathers on side of head next to braid.

4 For spear, use saved pointed end of craft pick. Cut a notch in cut end. Cut a ¼"x½" brown suede rectangle. Fringe one short side. Tie around spear. Glue feathers on suede. Glue spear on doll hand. ■

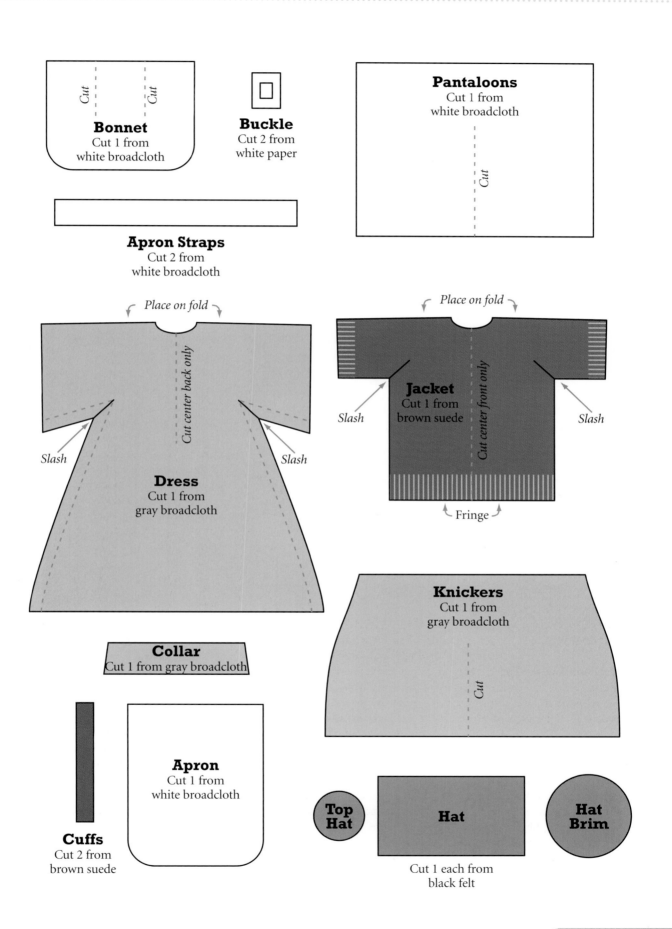

Bonnet
Cut 1 from
white broadcloth

Cut *Cut*

Buckle
Cut 2 from
white paper

Pantaloons
Cut 1 from
white broadcloth

Cut

Apron Straps
Cut 2 from
white broadcloth

Place on fold

Cut center back only

Slash

Slash

Dress
Cut 1 from
gray broadcloth

Place on fold

Slash

Jacket
Cut 1 from
brown suede

Cut center front only

Slash

Fringe

Knickers
Cut 1 from
gray broadcloth

Cut

Collar
Cut 1 from gray broadcloth

Cuffs
Cut 2 from
brown suede

Apron
Cut 1 from
white broadcloth

Top Hat

Hat

Hat Brim

Cut 1 each from
black felt

SNOWMAN CANDLE HOLDER

by Sandy Parpart

MATERIALS

- Two steel cans: 5¾" tall x 3½" wide; 2" tall x 2¾" wide
- Metal paint*: blue, white, black, red
- Paintbrushes: ¾" flat, ¼" stencil
- Sea sponge
- Decorative snow
- Felt: 4"x11½" red, scrap green
- Buttons: two ½" square gray, one ⅝" red shank
- Two 12mm moveable eyes
- Two 4" twigs
- Vinegar
- Block of wood to fit inside large can
- Candle to fit in small can
- Glue gun and glue sticks.
- Thick craft glue
- Craft stick, green thread, hammer, large nail, needle, paper plate, paper towels, pencil, ruler, sandpaper, scissors, tracing paper.

* The following products were used for this project: Deco Art™ No-Prep Metal Paint™ · Kunin Rainbow™ Felt · Loew-Cornell paintbrush.

INSTRUCTIONS

- ☺ Adult supervision is needed when working with hot glue gun.
- ☺ Trace and cut out pattern. Follow directions.
- ☺ Let paint dry completely after each coat.

1 Remove labels and glue from cans. Wash with warm soapy water, then vinegar. Rinse with water and dry cans thoroughly. Use sandpaper to sand sharp edges on inside edge of cans.

2 Paint 2 coats of blue paint on inside and outside of cans. Wet the sea sponge, then wring out as much water as possible. Dip sponge in white paint and dab on outside of cans, letting some blue show through.

3 Use glue gun to glue bottom of small can on top of large can. Use craft glue to glue vest on snowman body, overlapping in front. Insert block of wood into large can. Use hammer and nail to punch a hole on each side of snowman body 1½" from top. Remove wood. For arm, hold end of twig in hole and hot glue in place on inside of can. Hold until glue is set. Repeat for other arm.

4 For bow tie, cut green felt 2"x2½". Cut another piece ½"x1½". To make bow, gather stitch in center of large piece. Pull up gathers. Knot and clip thread. Glue small felt piece around middle of bow, overlapping ends. Glue bow on snowman. Glue buttons on vest.

5 Glue eyes on face with craft glue. For nose, glue red button nose on face with glue gun. For mouth, dip handle end of paintbrush in black paint and paint 4 dots under nose. To

Continued on next page.

dry brush red cheeks, dip stencil brush in paint. Dab on paper towel until brush is almost dry and paint cheeks. Add decorative snow on side of head, neck, arms, buttons, and bottom of snowman.

Insert candle in top can. ■

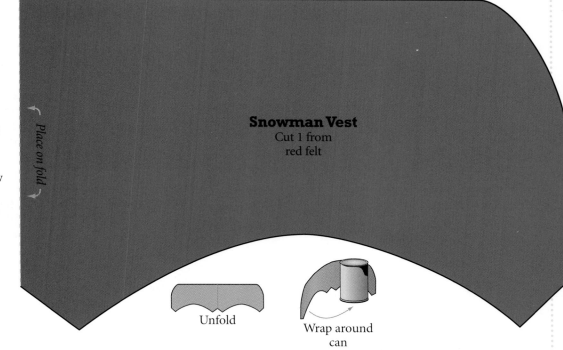

Place on fold

Snowman Vest
Cut 1 from
red felt

Unfold

Wrap around
can

SANTA SPOON ORNAMENT

by Helen Rafson

MATERIALS

► Craft spoon*
► White craft foam
► Acrylic paint*: white, black, light orange, red
► Black permanent fine-tip marker
► Pom poms: 5mm red, ¼" white
► Four ⅜" wide white buttons
► 7" length of gold cording
► Thick craft glue
► Paintbrush, tracing paper, pencil, ruler, scissors, toothpick

* The following products were used for this project: Forsters, Inc.® craft spoon· Aleene's Premium-Coat Acrylic Paint.

Mustache
Cut 1 from white foam

INSTRUCTIONS

☺ Trace and cut out patterns. Follow directions.
☺ Let paint dry between coats.

1 See Figure 1. Paint 2 coats of white on beard, hat trim, and eyebrows. Paint 2 coats of red on hat. Paint 2 coats of light orange on face.

2 Use marker to draw dash lines around beard, hat, trim, face, eyebrows, and mustache.

3 Dip handle end of paintbrush into black paint and make 2 eyes. Dip end of a toothpick into white paint and make highlights in eyes.

4 Glue on mustache, red pom pom for nose, and white pom pom for hat.

5 Glue buttons on beard. For hanger, fold cording in half. Glue cut ends on back of Santa's hat.

Option: To make into a pin, glue pinback on back of Santa. ■

Figure 1

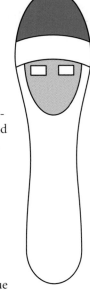

SANTA DOOR HANGER

by Debi Goldfisher

MATERIALS

- ▶ 3"x9½" wood door hanger
- ▶ Felt*: 5"x5" white, 4"x4" apricot, 8"x8" ruby, 3"x5" black
- ▶ Acrylic paint*: white, dark green
- ▶ Acrylic spray sealer
- ▶ Paintbrushes: #8 flat, #00 liner
- ▶ White embroidery floss
- ▶ 12" of ⅛" red ribbon
- ▶ Polyester fiberfill
- ▶ ⅜" red button
- ▶ Two 1" wrapped presents
- ▶ ½" white pom pom
- ▶ Three ½" gold jingle bells
- ▶ Thick craft glue
- ▶ Brown paper bag, needle, paper clip, paper plate, pencil, pinking shears, ruler, sandpaper, scissors, straight pins, toothpick, tracing paper

* The following products were used for this project: Kunin Classic Rainbow™ Felt · Plaid FolkArt® acrylic paint.

INSTRUCTIONS

☺ Trace and cut out patterns. Follow directions.

☺ Use two strands of white embroidery floss and a running stitch to sew all pieces together.

1 Sand door hanger. Paint front and edges with two coats dark green. Thin a little white with water to consistency of ink. Use liner brush to paint stitch lines around edges of doorknob opening and outside edges of hanger. Spray with a coat of acrylic sealer. Rub surface with a piece of paper bag to smooth.

2 Pin hat and face pieces together so straight edges are even. Use pinking shears to cut ⅞"x3" white hat band. Pin band over edges, slightly overlapping face. Stitch hat, band, and face together along center of hat band.

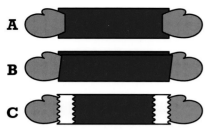

Figure 1

3 Use pinking shears to cut five 2" slits along lower edge of beard. Pin beard on front of face, leaving ⅜" of face exposed. Stitch upper edge of beard on face.

4 Pin face/hat/beard piece on head, wrong sides together. Stitch around outer edge of hat and face, leaving an opening for stuffing. Sew under beard so beard hangs loose. Stuff lightly with fiberfill. Sew opening closed. Sew bell on hat. Glue pom pom on hat, hiding bell stitches.

5 For eyes, glue beads on face, using toothpick to apply glue. For nose, glue red button under eyes.

6 For arms, cut two 2"x8" ruby strips. For cuffs, cut two ¾"x2" white strips. See Figure 1. Place a glove, with thumb up, at each end of one arm. Place other arm over first, sandwiching gloves between layers. Put a cuff on each end of arm, overlapping glove. Pin all layers together. Stitch together along edges, leaving an opening for stuffing. Stuff lightly, and sew closed.

7 Glue center of arms on bottom of hanger. When arms are folded, thumbs should be up and cuffs on outside. Glue head on hanger ½" above arms. Glue presents so they show above tops of folded arms. Wrap arms around presents. Overlap and glue gloves together. Use paper clip to hold hands together until glue dries.

8 Cut ribbon in half and thread each piece through a bell. Tie in a bow. Glue a bell on each upper corner of hanger. ■

To simplify this project for younger crafters, see page 14 for a no-sew method to make the Santa.

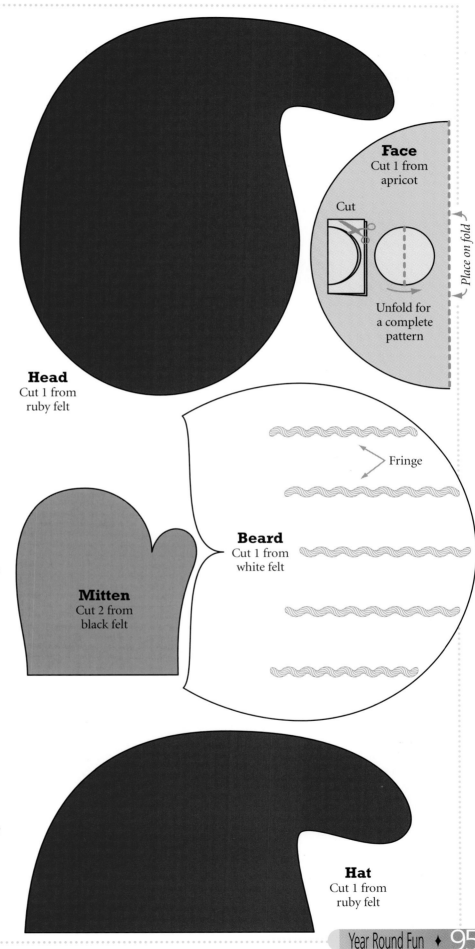

Face
Cut 1 from apricot

Cut

Place on fold

Unfold for a complete pattern

Head
Cut 1 from ruby felt

Fringe

Beard
Cut 1 from white felt

Mitten
Cut 2 from black felt

Hat
Cut 1 from ruby felt

HANUKKAH CARD HOLDER

by Gail Green

MATERIALS

- ▶ Craft foam: royal blue, light blue, white, brown, light green
- ▶ White dimensional paint*
- ▶ One 5mm black half-round bead
- ▶ ⅔ yard of ¼" gold satin ribbon
- ▶ Thick craft glue **Optional:** *Peel n stick™ double-sided adhesive*
- ▶ Hole punch, pencil, scissors, ruler, small paintbrush

* Shiny White Fashion® dimensional fabric paint from Plaid Enterprises, Inc. was used for this project.

INSTRUCTIONS

☺ Trace and cut out patterns. Follow directions.

1 From light blue foam, cut a 10"x12" rectangle for hanging and a 4"x10" piece for pocket. Run a thin bead of glue along both sides and bottom of pocket and press in place on bottom of hanging.

2 Center and glue one royal blue triangle on hanging ⅞" from top edge with one point down. Glue second triangle over first triangle, having top point extend 1" above edge of hanging.

3 Paint dove beak gold. Tie 6" length of ribbon in a bow. Glue dove in the following order: branch, dove body, wing, leaves, eye.

4 Punch two holes for hanger ½" from top and 1" from sides. Cut 18" length of ribbon. Thread ends of ribbon through holes from front to back. Tie knots in back.

5 Use white dimensional paint to write the word Shalom! on pocket. Let dry for 24 hours. ■

Dove Body
Cut 1 from
white foam

Branch
Cut 1 from
brown foam

SHALOM!

Dove Wing
Cut 2 from
white foam

Leaf
Cut 3 from
light green foam

Star of David
Cut 2 from
royal blue foam

MILK BOTTLE NATIVITY

by Terri Quillen

Christmas is a favorite time for decorating the home. Here's an inexpensive project that the whole family can work on together.

MATERIALS

- 2 half-pint white plastic "chug" milk bottles
- Felt*: antique gold, sky blue, dark brown, beige, ivory, white
- Foam shapes: 2" egg, 3" egg, 3" ball
- 1 lady's tan nylon stocking
- 8" of medium-brown mohair braided doll hair
- 10" of ¼" gold braided rope trim
- 4 black beaded pins
- 1 yard of beige wired paper ribbon
- One 20 mm natural wooden bead
- Gold metallic paint marker
- 18 yards gold pearl cotton
- 2½"x3" box, 1" deep
- 2" square of white cardboard
- 6" piece of cardboard
- Pink powdered makeup blush
- Glue gun & hot glue
- Compass, pinking shears, ruler, scissors

Kunin Felt was used in this project.

JOSEPH INSTRUCTIONS

☺ Adult supervision is needed when using a glue gun.

1 Cut a 2" x 11" strip from gold felt with pinking shears. Glue strip around base of bottle.

2 Cut an 11" circle from brown felt. Spread glue over mouth of bottle. Lay circle over mouth of bottle. Crimp felt down around neck. Spread glue over bottle. Crimp brown felt down into glue, finger gathering into soft folds as you go.

3 Cut a 4" square from stocking. Stretch it around long side of egg. Glue ends in back. Glue egg on top of bottle with narrow end pointing down and egg tilted at a 45° angle.

For eyes, insert two beaded pins into egg ¼" apart. Brush powdered makeup on cheeks.

4 For collar, cut 6" gold-rope trim. Wrap rope around neck, gluing ends together in back.

5 For sleeves, cut a 3"x12" strip from brown felt. Roll into a 1"x12" tube. Glue seam shut. Cut two hands from beige felt. Glue 1 hand inside one end of brown felt tube. Glue tube around back of robe, having one 3" arm on one side, leaving other long end of tube dangling.

6 For shepherd's rod, bend wired paper ribbon in three 9" lengths. Wrap ribbon around tripled section. Cut ribbon and glue end down. Bend uncut end in shape of a candy cane to resemble a rod.

7 Wrap dangling end of sleeve tube around shepherd's rod. Glue end of rod and end of tube on robe. Glue hand in place over rod.

8 Unbraid doll hair. Glue hair in an oval around face.

9 Cut the headdress pattern from brown felt. Place on top of head Fold sides down and around shoulders. Glue all folds in place.

10 Cut 9" from gold rope. Tie around top of head, over hair and over turban. Cross ends in back and glue in place.

MARY INSTRUCTIONS

1 Use pinking shears to cut a 2½"x12" strip from gold felt. Glue around base of bottle, folding along top edge to fit.

2 Use pinking shears to cut a 9" circle from blue felt. Spread glue around neck of bottle. Drape circle over neck off center, with one edge ¼" above bottom of bottle. This is the back. Fold felt around bottle neck.

3 Cut a 4" square of nylon from stocking. Stretch it around foam ball. Glue ends together. Glue ball centered on top of bottle with seam facing back. *Note: Do not face seam down on bottle neck or head will not rest properly.*

For eyes, insert two beaded pins

Hand
Cut 4 from
beige felt

into egg ¼" apart. Brush powdered makeup on cheeks.

4 For collar, cut a ¾"x6" piece of white felt. Fold in half hoizontally and glue around neck.

5 For headdress, cut a 1½"x5½" strip from blue felt. Glue strip across forehead. Cut an 8" square from blue felt. Fold in half diagonally in an irregular triangle. Glue on head over top edge of blue band of felt. Fold around head and glue down.

6 For sleeves, cut a 3¼"x9" strip from blue felt. Roll it into a 1¼"x9" tube. Glue seam shut. Cut 2 hands from beige felt. Glue a hand inside each end of tube.

7 Flip up back of blue felt head scarf. Wrap arms around doll. Glue arms in place at center back. Glue hands together in center front.

MANGER INSTRUCTIONS

1 Cut a 1"x11" strip of brown felt to cover sides of a 2½"x3" box. Glue felt on sides of box.

2 For straw, wrap pearl cotton 100 times around a 6" piece of cardboard. Remove from cardboard and tie strands tightly together in center with a 12" strand. Cut loops and trim ends evenly. Place in box.

Joseph Headdress
Cut 1 from
brown felt

BABY JESUS INSTRUCTIONS

1 Flatten pointed end of remaining foam egg. Glue bead to flat end.

2 Cut a 4" circle from ivory felt. Spread glue on round end of egg. Press felt on glue. Add more glue on edges of felt. Fold felt around egg.

3 Cut four ¾"x11" strips from white felt. Wrap strips around outside of egg for "swaddling." Glue ends down.

4 For halo, cut 1½" circle from white posterboard. Use gold marker to paint rays on circle. Glue on back of bead head. With markers, make two small black dots for eyes and two pink dots for cheeks. Lay Baby Jesus in manger. ◼

CHRISTMAS ORNAMENTS

by Lee Lindeman

CHRISTMAS TREE MATERIALS

► 1"x4"x6" plastic craft foam*
► 6"x8" green felt*
► 24 paper-covered wire ties
► Serrated knife
► Cord for hanger
► Thick craft glue
► Pencil, pinking shears, scissors, tracing paper

* The following products were used for this project: Styrofoam® plastic craft foam · Kunin felt.

CHRISTMAS TREE INSTRUCTIONS

☺ Adult supervision needed when using serrated knife.

☺ Trace and cut out pattern. Follow directions.

1 Use knife to cut tree from foam. Glue one felt tree on each side of foam.

2 Cut ties in half. Loosely coil each piece. Dip coils in glue and glue on front and back of tree. Uncoil some of the pieces a little, dip end in glue and poke into sides of tree.

3 For hanger, tie ends of cord together. Glue on top of tree.

STRING ORNAMENT INSTRUCTIONS

1 Dip toothpick in glue. Use toothpick to draw a design on ball. While glue is still wet, lay cord on glue lines. Continue until whole ball has been covered with cord design. Let dry.

2 Poke a hole at top of ball. Cut 10" cord for hanger. Dip ends in glue and insert in hole.

3 Tie ribbon in a bow. Trim ribbon ends at a slant. Glue on top of ball next to hanger.

STRING ORNAMENT MATERIALS

► 3" plastic craft foam ball*
► 48" red cord
► 12" of ⅝" red ribbon
► Thick craft glue
► Toothpick

* Styrofoam® plastic craft foam was used for this project.

SNOWMAN ORNAMENT MATERIALS

▶ 3" plastic craft foam ball*
▶ Craft foam*: white, black, red, green, yellow, pink, orange
▶ Hole punch
▶ 14" green ribbon
▶ 12" gold cord
▶ Fine-line permanent black marker
▶ Thick craft glue
▶ Pencil, scissors, tracing paper

The following products were used for this project: Styrofoam® plastic craft foam · Westrim craft foam.

SNOWMAN ORNAMENT INSTRUCTIONS

☺ Trace and cut out patterns. Follow directions.

1 See photo. Glue shapes on ball. Use black marker to draw snowman faces and buttons. Glue stars on top and bottom of ball. Punch out 40 white foam dots. Glue randomly above snowmen.

2 Poke a hole at top of ball, through star. Dip ends of cord in glue and insert in hole. Tie ribbon in a bow. Trim ends at a slant. Glue on top of ball near hanger. ■

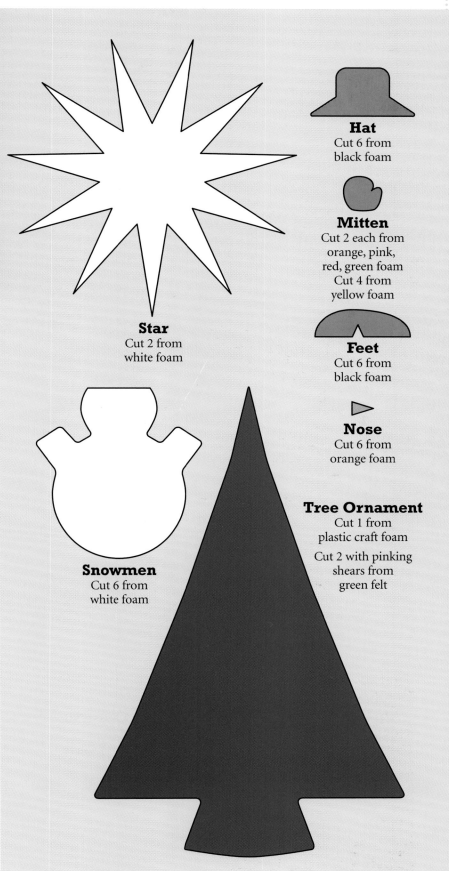

Star
Cut 2 from white foam

Hat
Cut 6 from black foam

Mitten
Cut 2 each from orange, pink, red, green foam
Cut 4 from yellow foam

Feet
Cut 6 from black foam

Nose
Cut 6 from orange foam

Tree Ornament
Cut 1 from plastic craft foam
Cut 2 with pinking shears from green felt

Snowmen
Cut 6 from white foam

SANTA RING TOSS GAME

by Lisa Marto Weber

MATERIALS

- ► 10"x11½" popcorn can
- ► 3 lb. coffee can
- ► 2 lb. coffee can
- ► 8" diameter plastic funnel
- ► Acrylic paint*: red, burgundy, white, light blue, flesh, pink, gold
- ► Gloss varnish
- ► Paintbrushes: 1½" round, ¼" flat
- ► Sponge
- ► Two 9"x12" pieces antique white felt*
- ► 1½" giant art punch heart*
- ► Paper edgers*: Seagull
- ► Pinking shears
- ► Craft foam: white (2¾"x2¾", 2"x32", 1½"x22"), black (2"x32"), green (scrap), red (scrap)
- ► Chenille stems: 6 red, 6 white
- ► 96" of pine garland
- ► Thirty 1" white pom poms
- ► Black fine-line marker
- ► Glue gun & glue sticks
- ► Graphite paper, pencil, scissors, foam plate

* The following products were used for this project: DecoArt® Americana Acrylic Paints ·

INSTRUCTIONS

☺ Trace and cut out patterns. Follow directions.

☺ Let paint dry between coats.

1 Remove all labels. Wash and dry cans.

2 Paint large can, medium can, and funnel red. For head, paint small can flesh. For nose, paint heart flesh. Transfer eye patterns onto small can.

Go over lines with black marker. Paint eyes following painting guide. Sponge paint cheeks and top of nose with pink. Paint buckle gold.

3 Sponge on burgundy in a random pattern on red cans and funnel.

4 Use edgers to cut 2"x32" white foam strip for bottom of coat. Glue in place. Cut a 1½"x12" strip of white foam for fur center on coat.

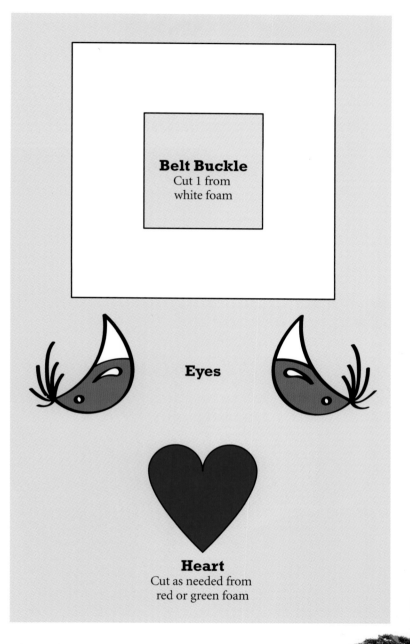

Belt Buckle
Cut 1 from
white foam

Eyes

Heart
Cut as needed from
red or green foam

Glue in place, having the top of strip fold over top of can about 2 inches. Cut a second strip 6" long and glue on other red can. For belt, cut a 2"x32" black strip. Glue around can. Glue belt on center front of belt.

5 For beard, cut five 1"x14" felt strips using pinking shears. Fold strips in half and glue on face for bottom layer, making strips slightly shorter on sides. Cut three 1"x10" strips and glue above 1st row. For mustache, cut two ½"x8" strips and glue above 2nd row on each side.

Glue two ½"x4" strips between them. Glue four ½"x6" strips on each side of nose. Glue heart nose over mustache.

6 For hair, cut small ½" strips of felt and glue under funnel. Glue pom poms around the brim of funnel and one on top.

7 Make rings from garland, chenille, or both. For chenille rings, twist red and white chenille together to look like candy canes. Wrap ends

together. For garland rings, cut 18 pieces. Overlap ends and twist to form rings. Cut hearts from red or green foam and glue on ring. ■

This Santa ring toss game can be stored within itself. The rings will fit inside the small can, and the cans fit inside one another. This is a great activity for school functions and special days around the holidays. Make or buy small prizes for kids to win if they get a ring around Santa's hat.

MILK BOTTLE SNOWMAN

by Sandy Parpart

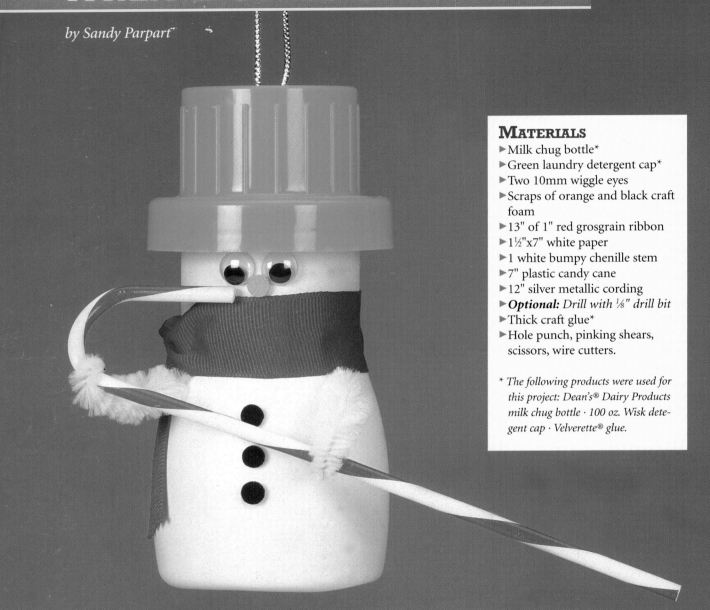

MATERIALS
- ▶ Milk chug bottle*
- ▶ Green laundry detergent cap*
- ▶ Two 10mm wiggle eyes
- ▶ Scraps of orange and black craft foam
- ▶ 13" of 1" red grosgrain ribbon
- ▶ 1½"x7" white paper
- ▶ 1 white bumpy chenille stem
- ▶ 7" plastic candy cane
- ▶ 12" silver metallic cording
- ▶ *Optional: Drill with ⅛" drill bit*
- ▶ Thick craft glue*
- ▶ Hole punch, pinking shears, scissors, wire cutters.

* The following products were used for this project: Dean's® Dairy Products milk chug bottle · 100 oz. Wisk detergent cap · Velverette® glue.

INSTRUCTIONS

1 Tie ends of silver cord in knot. Trim ends. Glue on center top of detergent cap. **Option:** *Drill 2 holes next to each other in center top of detergent cap. Push silver metallic cording down one hole and up other. Tie ends in knot. Trim ends.*

2 For hat, glue cap over top of bottle. For face, glue white paper over green bottom part of cap. Tie red ribbon around snowman's neck, making sure to cover edge of paper. Slide knot to side of neck and glue to keep it in place. Trim scarf ends with pinking shears, or use regular scissors and trim ends at a slant. Glue scarf ends on snowman body.

3 For arms, use wire cutters to cut two 3¼" pieces of chenille stem. Cut between bumps. To attach arms, use pointed scissors to carefully poke 2 small holes in snowman body just under the scarf and towards the front. Glue chenille stems in holes.

4 For buttons, punch 3 black foam circles and glue on front of snowman body. For nose, punch 1 orange foam circle and glue just above scarf. Glue eyes above nose.

5 To make snowman hold candy cane, wrap one arm around from below candy cane. Wrap other arm around from above candy cane. ◼